STRESS MANAGEMENT MADE EASY

About the author

Mike Levy is a freelance journalist living in Cambridge and is married with two grown-up children. He is a regular contributor to magazines such as *Director* (for the Institute of Directors), *Conference and Incentive Travel*, *Business*, *Training Journal*, *Education Computing & Technology* and many others.

He is the author of several business books including *Presentations Made Easy* for Law Pack, *Success in Marketing* for David Grant Publishing and books for Gower Publishing. He is currently working on a book on creative problem solving in business. He is a freelance press officer, copywriter and playwright (specialising in commemorative plays and events). He is also developing a new consultancy, 'Cambridge Thinking Solutions.' You can contact him by email: mike.levy@ntlworld.com or via his website www.mikelevy.co.uk.

Stress Management Made Easy
by Mike Levy
with Roy Bailey

Copyright 2001 Law Pack Publishing Limited

LAWPACK™

10–16 Cole Street London SE1 4YH
www.lawpack.co.uk
All rights reserved.

ISBN 1 902646 79 7

Table of contents

Acknowledgements

The author would like to thank all the people who have helped in the preparation of this book, especially Dr. Roy Bailey (author of several works on stress management including *The Gower Stress Management Toolkit for Trainers and Counsellors 2001*) and the many members of the on-line discussion group for Human Resources professionals, UKHRD serviced by Fenman Ltd.

Roy Bailey PhD MA DACP Dip EHP NLP RT(Cert.) FCIPD is a Consultant and Chartered Clinical Psychologist, NLP Mentor, Lead Management Consultant, Trainer, Personal Therapist and Counsellor.

A Fellow of the Chartered Institute for Personnel and Development, Roy is a leading international figure in the fields of stress management, counselling at work and managerial mentoring. He is also a Managing Director of 'CSL Ltd', the Psychology and Medico-Legal Company, and Managing Director of the Centre for Personal Excellence. Visiting Professor of Managerial Psychology at The International Management Centres - Europe, Roy provides psychological services to trainers, counsellors, managers and employees throughout Europe. He is the author of many resources on stress management and counselling such as Gower's *Stress Management Toolkit for Trainers and Counsellors*, *Activities for Managing Stress* and the companion manual *50 Activities for Developing Counselling Skills*.

Thanks to The Holst Group for information on the McQuaig Word Survey and MOT.

Introduction

There is nothing new about stress at work. It's been around ever since man and woman first realised they had to put effort into feeding, housing and clothing themselves. Techniques for dealing with stress are equally timeless: from pills, potions and palliatives to incantations, prayer and ritual. Using drugs to take away the symptoms of stress is equally nothing new. In the last century, opium (usually in the form of a laudanum elixir) was widely used as a stress-reliever:

Laudanum gave me repose - how divine that repose is.

S.T. Coleridge

Opium use was made unlawful in the 19th century, mainly because of the effects it had on people's attitudes to hard grind. The authorities were worried it would make workers too stress free and result in them working less hard. People have always had their own ways of dealing with the problem. These days, some people are likely to turn to tobacco and alcohol for relief of stress symptoms. Others may seek a variety of other options including going for invigorating walks, taking warm baths or rigorous exercise.

Just as stress is an ancient problem, so is pressure. But there is a distinct difference between stress and pressure. Pressure is what many of us feel every day in work: the pressure to meet deadlines, catch a meeting, fulfil an order or complete a tax return. Pressure is the fuel that keeps the engine of work going. Pressure can be challenging, it can be fun and it can be highly rewarding. Without pressure, things don't get done; there is little impetus to do anything well and on time. Pressure is part of our everyday work and home experience.

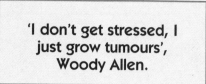

'I don't get stressed, I just grow tumours', Woody Allen.

However, stress is different. Stress can be harmful and destructive. It can cause illness, suffering and depression. In some people it can be negative and costly - a barrier to efficiency and a drain on our resources, personally, physically and financially. Stress and pressure are two completely different phenomena: stress in some people should be avoided and minimised; but pressure can be good - a challenge that has to be met - even, sometimes, encouraged. But although pressure can be good, it can easily turn into something much more harmful and negative: stress.

In this book, we will be covering the methods designed to help you become a more effective stress manager.

Think icon - wherever you see this sign - stop, pause and think about your own situation.

What is stress?

Chapter 1

What is stress?

What you'll find in this chapter:

- ➡ **Defining stress**
- ➡ **Predicting key stressors**
- ➡ **Calculating the impact of stress**
- ➡ **The long-term effects of stress**

Stress management is a fundamental part of everyday human resource management. If you are responsible for staff, their well-being and effectiveness at work, then stress is an issue that should concern you.

> Stress is a part of our job. I pay my staff well and expect them to take all the stresses and strains that come our way. If they don't like the heat, get out of the kitchen, I say.
>
> Senior partner in an accountancy practice

The quotation above is not untypical of senior managers in this country, especially of the older school of people management. 'I pay, therefore you suffer' is a long-held view among many bosses, especially if they have worked themselves up the company. Stress is seen as a good test of character, a necessary (and often sufficient) condition of a successful company.

Yet this view is short-sighted. Performance and stress are not always compatible. This is not to say, however, that it is your job to remove all signs of stress at work. 'The concept of an appropriate amount of stress is important', say Kast and Rosenzweig in *Organisation and Management* (McGraw-Hill, 1985). Appropriate stress is that level of stress which induces maximum performance in individuals. Their view, based on much research, is that:

- Too little stress: people 'rust out' with boredom and under-stimulation.

- Too much stress: people 'burn out' with too much to do.

They say that there is an optimum range of stress, where the positive aspects outweigh the negative. Each individual, they say, has an 'optimum range' of stress and it is management's role to ensure that it maintains an equilibrium within this range.

Defining stress - not an easy task

How do we define 'stress'? This is a complex area; not so simple as it first appears. Stress cannot be simply listed as a group of causes to which straightforward solutions can be applied. It is not a matter of taking an appropriate 'stressor' from a list and applying a given remedy. Would that it were that simple. Nor is there any consensus over the root causes and hence appropriate interventions for stress at work.

We don't all react to the same stressor in the same way. It's not just that we may perceive a stressor differently to our colleagues, but we may also react in a totally different way. Take, for example, a noisy factory. Person A might easily see the noise as highly annoying, painful even, certainly stressful. So might Person B. But Person C might like noise, enjoy the hubbub, and revel in the cover it gives him or her to talk to friends. Person A and B (both prone to disliking noise) might well react in different ways: Person A becomes irritable and depressed, internalises the stress; Person B just gets angry and aggressive.

Another view of stress is that it is physiological and goes back to our Stone-Age ancestry. This approach focuses on the familiar fight-flight-freeze response. When we are stressed some of us might experience an innate need to stay and fight the fear, run away from it or become temporarily incapacitated (unable to act or think clearly).

Much depends on what type of people we are, how we appraise a stressful situation, and what coping methods we bring to bear on the problem.

Another view of stress - a more up to date one - is the so-called 'transactional approach'. This puts the victim in a more dynamic role. Dealing with stress is like a transaction - the way we deal with it depends on supply and demand: the demands imposed by the stressful event (real or perceived) in relation to the supply of our resources to cope. If the supply of coping resources is greater than the demands made, there will not be a negative stress reaction. But if the demands made exceed our resources to cope, all kinds of stressful outcomes may occur.

Perceptions are as important as reality: the threat of a meeting with the boss may be more stressful than the actual event; the thought of a change in working methods may be more harmful than the change process itself.

The key point is that individuals perceive events in different ways. One person may see a change in working methods as an exciting prospect; another as a deeply stressful life event.

The great strength about the transactional approach is that it allows us to pursue stress as people managers: assessing the abilities and strengths of our workforce, and evaluating the potential for a situation to become stressful.

One valuable lesson is that it is not always so easy to predict when exactly pressure becomes stress. It is a very individual thing - and what is stimulating pressure for one person may be overwhelming stress for another. It also varies for the same person over time:

> When I feel well and things are going fine at home, I can cope with any amount of pressure at work. But if things are going badly, the kids are sick, the dog is ill and my husband is driving me mad, then the smallest amount of pressure at work becomes so stressful.
>
> Barbara Kenton, company PA

An unrealistic challenge, a destructive relationship at work, work schedules and job demands that cannot be met without injury to our physical or mental well-being: this is stress. There is now quite an industry dealing with the effects of stress on the mind and body. The aim, usually, is to convert stress into normal work pressure. Therapists use a variety of techniques to help individuals cope with work-related stress. One of these is 'positive memory', where you are encouraged to think of a happy, life-enhancing memory whenever you feel overwhelmed by stress. A similar approach is 'positive imaging', where you are directed by the therapist to look at the best-case scenario. When we are stressed it is too easy to take the overwhelmingly negative viewpoint - to see everything in terms of black and grey. Positive imaging encourages individuals to think about the good things that can come out of any situation.

Yet another technique is Edward de Bono's 'Six Thinking Hats'. De Bono's technique involves thinking through a problem in a disciplined, sequenced way. For instance, discussion should first look only at positive aspects of a solution - the so-called 'Yellow Hat' approach - then, quite separately, the negative aspects - Black Hat - and so on. This disciplined thinking skill is aimed at encouraging you to think through issues in a highly ordered and logical way - rather than as a gut-reaction panic. Like many other stress techniques, it is a series of signposts that lead you towards a healthier work experience. Other methods used by stress counsellors and therapists include various forms of neuro-muscular relaxation techniques. These often involve the tensing and relaxation of muscles and various yoga-like exercises aimed at slowing and deepening breathing and the relaxation of muscles. Some therapists use role-play exercise. In acting out stressful situations, it is thought that people can better face their problems, develop coping strategies or understand more about what motivates other people to become sources of stress. Therapists may also use various forms of regression analysis, taking their clients back through their lives to see where the first danger signals of stress appeared.

We think of our lives as a series of traffic lights. As a therapist I am used to dealing with people who have already reached red for danger. What I do is take them back through their experiences to find out where and when the green changed to amber - in other words, where the first signs of stress started to emerge.

Bob Goldberg, stress counsellor

One of the key signposts that may be discovered is the time when the person first started to ignore the stressors in his or her life.

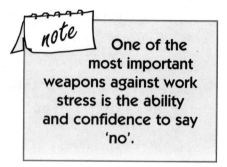

One of the most important weapons against work stress is the ability and confidence to say no. People in the workplace need to be assertive enough to put their work demands in a priority order. There are times when you need to say, 'No, I can't stay on for an extra hour at work, I need to go to the gym'. But someone who can say that is not only assertive and confident; they are much more self-aware than many of us. They have the ability to recognise when pressure turns to stress. They can judge when it is right to refuse to take more stress.

Bob Goldberg

Whenever I am asked to stay late at work, I try to calculate in my head the costs and benefits of doing so. The cost may be a lost jogging session or a swim in the local pool, and the effect of missing that may make me less well or prone to illness. The impact of that on my work is then much more damaging than missing an extra hour of work.

Jim Fletcher, teacher

Jim's confidence in being able to 'calculate' the stress impact of an extra hour's work is also matched by his status and ability to say 'no' to the boss. In this case, individual stress avoidance comes down to being aware of potential stressors and the case for refusing to become more stressed.

If I really can't convince the boss that my missing a meeting will do the school more good than harm in the end, then I have to find ways of compensating myself. An extra two hours of stress at a meeting might be matched by an extra visit to the swimming pool.

Jim Fletcher

In terms of long-term benefits, you might like to think about:

- taking a relaxing massage or an aromatherapy course;

- yoga or meditation;

- taking up a new sport, or rekindling an interest in one;

- regular exercise;

- getting away more often for the weekend (without the mobile phone);

- taking your holiday entitlements (all of them).

> **?** How might you compensate yourself for an extra stressful period? The usual stress 'escapes' such as alcohol, tobacco and chocolate may give you a short-term buzz, but they do nothing to alleviate the long-term effects that stress could have on your physical and mental well-being. Indeed, all the evidence points to them doing more harm than good in terms of chronic heart disease, cancer and weight-gains.

Why you should take stress at work seriously

2

Chapter 2

Why you should take stress at work seriously

What you'll find in this chapter:

- ➠ Studies of stress in the work place
- ➠ The impact of stress on business
- ➠ Stress in the courts
- ➠ Legal responsibility of employers

It is easy to generalise about stress. As it is quite difficult to measure accurately, the phenomenon has a 'now you see it, now you don't' quality. But in the last few years, as the subject has been taken more seriously, detailed studies of stress in the population have been carried out. One such study was reported in the publication *Stress News*:

Professor Andy Smith and his team at Bristol University have been carrying out a survey into the prevalence of stress at work, under contract to the Health and Safety Executive. This is the first such study conducted within the general population...In this study, a 32-page questionnaire, after piloting, was sent out to a sample of 17,000 people randomly selected from the electoral register in the Bristol area. A response rate of 49 per cent included 4,135 people then in employment, whose responses to questions about work-related and general stress were analysed in detail; 20 per cent of this group of working people described themselves as 'very' or 'extremely' stressed at work on a multiple-choice scale.

Only 17 per cent of this high-stress-at-work group reported feeling similarly high levels of stress outside of their workplace, although they were more likely to consume more alcohol than they had done previously, and were less likely to do vigorous exercise. Perceived stress at work was also associated with reports of exposure to noise, high workload and lack of support. Those with high levels of reported stress at work also reported more frequent minor physical symptoms of ill-health and problems with mental health (within a population generally rating themselves as in quite good health).

Other evidence to show that stress at work is a big issue for business:

- Stress at work in the USA has been cited as costing over $150 billion a year.

- The cost of stress at work to UK industry has been estimated by the Chartered Institute of Personnel and Development (CIPD) to range from £5 billion to £11 billion.

- In as early as 1984, the Control Data Corporation (a major player in the IT world in the 80s, but now largely defunct) analysed the medical claims of their employees and discovered that, on average, an unhealthy employee cost $509 more than a healthy employee did for that year. They also found that their employees who were identified and designated as high risk had a 5 per cent higher absenteeism rate than their low-risk employees.

- Replacing a manager who is under-performing from stress at work can cost up to 90 per cent of their first annual salary for the replacement.

- Recent nationwide surveys by advertising agency D'Arcy, Masius, Benton & Bowles indicate that 75 per cent of all Americans say that their jobs cause them stress.

- A survey of people working in the City of London found that 65 per cent considered stress to be their primary health concern.

- *The Employment Gazette* recently claimed that of 328 million working days lost to industry, 111 million of these (just under a third) were associated with stress.

- *The Economist* magazine has proposed that as much as 2 per cent of the UK's Gross National Product is lost through stress-related problems.

- *The Economist* has also gone so far as to suggest that misuse of alcohol accounts for 33 per cent of work absences, and that 75 per cent of alcoholics remain in their jobs.

 In 1996, The Trades Union Congress (TUC) carried out a major survey on stress at work as reported by safety representative officers in UK companies. It concluded that occupational stress is the major health and safety issue in British workplaces, affecting workers in all sectors, regardless of company size.

The most commonly reported concern, occupational stress and overwork, clearly affected workers in all sizes of firm, both in the public as well as the private sectors. The TUC survey also analysed the jobs most likely to cause stress.

Breaking the responses down by industrial sector showed that the public sector has higher levels of stress than the private sector, suggesting that the impact of years of public sector cuts has left workforces demoralised and under pressure. However, other sectors show severe cause for concern too.

Stress in the courts

One reason why the whole stress issue at work has become more acute is the recent history of litigation. In 1994, there was the first successful case of a compensation payout against an employer for psychological stress caused by working conditions. The case sent shock waves throughout industry.

John Walker, a social services officer, sought £200,000 damages from Northumberland County Council after suffering two nervous breakdowns at work. The High Court held that an employer's duty to provide a safe working environment could be applied to mental, in addition to physical, injury.

John Walker won that case and it set alarm bells ringing in every boardroom in the country. The test case meant that employers are legally liable for creating unnecessary stress.

Another recent test case was that of a teacher who took her employers to court for causing classroom stress. The court found that her employer was indeed liable and that stress was an occupational health hazard. She won £47,000 in an out-of-court payment.

According to the UK Institute of Directors (IoD), there is an increasing 'compensation culture' - a dangerous turn for businesses who may stand to lose hundreds of thousands of pounds in litigation against them. The CBI (Confederation of British Industry) is equally concerned.

People are more aware of stress and put it as a label for all the things they find uncomfortable at work... Employers take stress very seriously and it has been identified as a cause of serious absence from work. This puts extra stress on colleagues too... The employer has to take the place of the family support unit. Employers want to do this because they need creative, energetic and innovative people in this competitive world. The systems to develop this need to be tailored to the individual, who may come to work with all sorts of stress-related problems. There is a need for a partnership between employers and other support agencies.

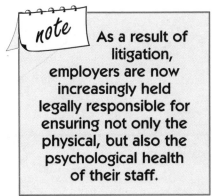

note

As a result of litigation, employers are now increasingly held legally responsible for ensuring not only the physical, but also the psychological health of their staff.

Janet Ascherson, Head of the Group for Environmental Health and Safety, CBI

Therefore, there is an increasingly active role for employers and managers in employee stress issues. Employers, certainly the good ones, are not washing their hands and saying, 'Stress comes with the job...it's the employees' business to cope with it as best they can'. This view has been shown by experts to be out of date and of little practical use to concerned managers.

What causes stress?

Chapter 3

What causes stress?

If you are a manager looking after people in your organisation the answer to the question, 'What causes stress at work' may be unpalatable: the chief cause may be you or other managers. The TUC survey asked safety reps to identify the chief causes of stress at work. The biggest single cause was identified as 'new management techniques'. These include quality circles and performance-related pay schemes. The TUC's view is that these new techniques can limit a trade union's ability to defend members from unreasonable demands made by management. Rather than negotiating changes with unions, managers may impose the changes, which makes the individual employees feel undervalued and without any influence over their work patterns.

Another cause of stress identified by safety reps included long hours. Transport rated highest in the long hours stakes, with 46 per cent of respondents citing hours of work as a main concern.

Long and stress-inducing working hours seem to be a peculiarly British phenomenon. According to the TUC 1996 report, 'previous TUC research has shown that British workers work longer hours than most other European workers, and that, against the trend, the working week in Britain is actually getting longer'. Whether the recently enacted European Working Time Directive will have any effect remains to be seen. It came into UK law in 1998 and says that each worker is entitled to certain basic rights including rest breaks at work, a minimum daily rest of 11 hours per day (for drivers and long shift workers), an average working week of under 48 hours and a minimum of 3 weeks' paid leave. If longer hours are required by an employer, they can be negotiated individually with an employee (see www.dti.gov.uk for more information).

Key causes of stress reported by TUC safety reps:

(Percentage of safety reps reporting each factor as a cause of stress in their workplace)

new management techniques 48%
long hours 31%
redundancies 24%
harassment 21%
shift work 16%
bullying 14%

Note: percentages do not total 100% because more than one answer could be given.

The TUC findings make an interesting comparison with a study carried out in a department of a US federal agency in 1985. A group of employees was asked to identify work stressors and the following results ensued:

Sources of work stress (in declining order of frequency reported)

1. unrealistic time lines
2. lack of clear direction
3. lack of recognition
4. unrealistic workloads
5. unresolved conflicts
6. interruptions
7. duplicating machine
8. having decisions overturned
9. lack of communication
10. personality conflicts
11. telephone problems
12. arbitrary decisions
13. lack of independence
14. lack of co-operation
15. money
16. disorganisation
17. being made fun of

(Source: Lawrence R. Murphy and Joseph J. Hurrell Jr., 'Stress Management Interventions at Work', ed. Cary Cooper, *Journal of Management Psychology*, vol ii, no. 1, 1987.)

What is clear from the above study and the TUC report (whether you agree with it in full or not) is that stress is clearly perceived as a major cause of organisational 'sickness'. And if they are right, management may be to blame for much of it. They cite 'new management

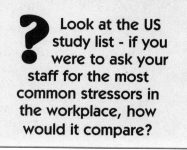

techniques' as the most reported cause of workplace stress. In the US study, 'money' comes way down the list of reported stressors: issues that are fundamentally the responsibility of management come highest. 'Unrealistic time lines' was almost three times more frequently cited than the next category - setting deadlines is primarily the work of managers.

As we said in the introduction, stress is nothing new. But according to Professor Cary Cooper of the University of Manchester,

Jobs these days are much more insecure; the UK has the longest working hours in Europe; downsizing, rightsizing or delayering (euphemisms for cutting costs by making employees redundant) have meant there are fewer people in the working environment which means that work loads are much more intense; IT and the internet have put extra stress on people.

Quoted from BBC Radio 4 series, 'You and Yours', 3/4/00

Another problem identified by Professor Cooper is the absence of 'natural counsellors' - (neighbours, family) - the social support system we used to turn to for help.

So although stress is nothing new, the evidence seems to be that stress at work is getting worse. This, of course, is of great concern to the individual suffering the symptoms of stress. It is also felt by the business organisation employing the stressed individuals, as this relates to whether the company has good people management. Any responsible manager has a duty to ensure that the well-being of staff is not harmed.

Stress is your business

If you are a manager, employee stress (and your own) is your business. This is because work-related stress can lead to a real reduction in your organisation's bottom line.

Confederation of British Industry (CBI) statistics from 1998 show that sickness absence accounts for 197 million lost days per year. They estimate a total cost to British industry of £11 billion. Within this figure, they say, the cost of stress-related absence is estimated at £7 billion per year.

Ill-health absence costs the individual employer dear, according to John Humphreys, head of Occupational Health and On-line Health Business at the consultancy William M. Mercer, based in Chichester:

> Where an employer relies on permanent health insurance the costs borne by the employer and insurer together at the end of two years is a staggering £76,750.
>
> *Stress News*, vol xi, no. 3, 1999

Stressed employees are more difficult to manage and it can be almost impossible to foster co-operative team building if some members of your staff are suffering from stress.

We tried to establish a daily team talk - a way of starting the day so that everyone could have their say about improving quality. But it just became another burden for many of our staff. Quality was the management's issue, not theirs, they said. Building up a team approach to continuous improvement was a waste of time while many staff felt too much stress at work. I think managers should beware of the 'straw on the camel's back' syndrome. I have learnt that it's only when our staff feel they can cope with work and they are happy that I can introduce initiatives successfully.

Graham Riley, MD of an engineering company

note

High levels of work-related stress are associated with low output, increased absenteeism and real production losses. It can lead to employees being tired, lacking in energy and mildly depressed. Some may become aggressive and more argumentative. Some experts claim that high levels of mental stress can weaken the immune system, making employees more prone to sickness and disease.

High levels of stress can lead to action being taken against an organisation for breaches of the health and safety laws. There is an increasing tendency for employees to sue employers for imposing levels of 'unfair stress'.

Stress prevention can help workers to be much more prepared for organisational change.

Watch out for the following symptoms of a stressed organisation:

- a higher than expected death rate from heart disease and cancer;

- more long-term sickness involving the heart or blood pressure;

- an increase in the number of staff seeking early retirement;

- a rise in the frequency and duration of industrial disputes;

- worsening punctuality records;

- a rise in the number of disciplinary cases each year.

> **?** Think about your members of staff that report to you. Do you notice any changes in their mood, health or attitude of late?

Do you keep a record of short-term absences? Has there been any rise in the number of people who may be suffering from stress or stress-related illness?

If you don't have good personnel records to hand, or haven't noticed whether anyone's behaviour has changed for the worse, then now is the time to start putting stress awareness on your agenda. It's a question of sharpening up your observation skills to notice whether your staff are as sharp, healthy, energetic and keen as before.

> I've always thought of stress as being a bit airy-fairy - a kind of weakness that you don't admit to. Also, it can be seen as a sign of hard work and diligence.
>
> Mary Keenan, CEO of a catering company

Mary's comments are not untypical of many managers and senior executives today. Stress is sometimes seen as a weakness, something we don't admit to - a sign that 'we can't take the heat of the kitchen'. But the question really is, 'does the kitchen really have to be so hot?'

Action plan

Short term

Look at your records of absence. Look for patterns, trends and reasons. Are there recurring illnesses and are these of the stress-related type: high blood pressure, headaches and backaches, exhaustion and being prone to viral infections?

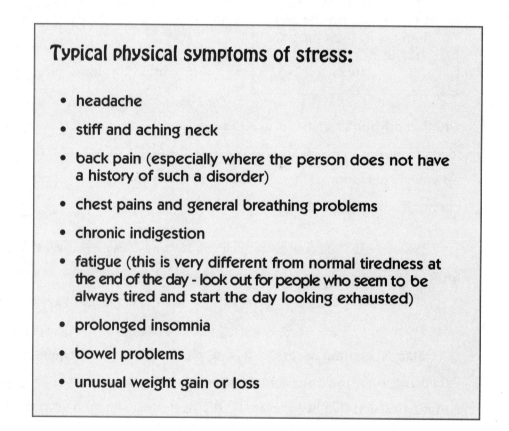

Typical physical symptoms of stress:

- headache

- stiff and aching neck

- back pain (especially where the person does not have a history of such a disorder)

- chest pains and general breathing problems

- chronic indigestion

- fatigue (this is very different from normal tiredness at the end of the day - look out for people who seem to be always tired and start the day looking exhausted)

- prolonged insomnia

- bowel problems

- unusual weight gain or loss

This is not a complete list. The key is to be aware of any unusual changes in employees' physical health. Managers, who know their staff well, will be able to spot any unusual changes in their well-being and physical health.

The key is to be aware of any unusual changes in employees' physical health.

It all started a few months after we had re-organised the office and changed a lot of working practices. At first I didn't notice that my secretary was taking increasing amounts of time off work for headaches and nausea - stuff that you couldn't put down to any one illness. She has always been incredibly loyal and hard working but I have to say it took me ages to realise that something was wrong. It was only after a year or so of these bouts of illness that I decided to have a chat to her, to see if anything was wrong at work or home that might be causing these aches and pains. After a bit of reluctance to talk, she eventually told me that the office re-organisation last year had really upset her. She felt less in control and a bit overlooked - having to do a lot more work when she didn't really believe it was worthwhile. I did know that she didn't agree with the changes we made but it never clicked that this was linked to her bouts of illness and absence. Things are much better for both of us now. We talked about the changes in office practice and I made sure her views were taken into account. We made a few minor changes but above all she now feels valued again. Her stress-related illnesses have all but disappeared, there's a much more co-operative atmosphere around and I have learnt a valuable lesson.

Marcia D, account manager for a law practice

Psychological effects of stress:

Look out for signs of:

- increased aggressive behaviour;

- mood swings;

- people finding it hard to concentrate;

- staff taking time off for such reasons as depression, unexplained fatigue, sudden phobias and neuroses;

- people becoming more morose and easily upset;

- people losing their sense of humour or sense of perspective on life;

- staff who are normally fairly calm suddenly becoming panic-stricken or taking a heavily pessimistic outlook on life;

- employees breaking into tears or not being able to cope with face-to-face meetings.

The presence (or absence) of the above signs should not in itself be sufficient grounds for suspecting stress. The key is to keep your eyes and all other senses open. Remember, you are a people manager, not a medical doctor. These signs and symptoms may be caused by other underlying medical conditions, and remember that it is rarely a case of just spotting stressors and matching symptoms to them. We all react in different ways depending on our physical and mental make-up, the circumstances of our environment and a whole host of intangibles (which may include how we feel on a grey day or what domestic concerns are troubling us). Psychologists also divide up behaviours into Type A and Type B.

Type A and Type B people

People displaying Type A behaviour are naturally movers and shakers. They like to compete; they enjoy a challenge and need to feel in control. They are often easily upset if their plans are disturbed.

Type B behaviour is calm, easy going and much less easily stressed, less obsessed about control and much more attracted to models of the 'easy life'. It is too simplistic to divide up the nation into Type A and Type B people. We are all mixtures of both types but those people whose Type A behaviour dominates may be more prone to stress when things don't go their way.

Spend time looking carefully at staff files and appraisal reports. Are some of your staff showing signs of stress? If so, is there some type of pattern: time of year; related to work carried out; related to some key change such as relocation, new job design, change of work rates expected or change in working conditions?

Sharpen up your listening and observation skills. An employee's stress will usually present itself in some tangible way sooner or later. Look out especially for changes of mood that can't easily be explained. Think about recent times when you have had to follow up complaints about an employee's work standard. Could it be stress-related?

Long term

Carry out a full 'stress audit' to discover the root causes of stress and the potential for problems and challenges to come. Being forewarned is an essential part of any effective manager's 'toolkit'.

The first question any manager should ask when dealing with workplace stress is, 'What do I need to know?'. This is true before any kind of stress auditing. It is of little value to ask a series of random questions about stress without thinking through your objectives. The key objective is to throw light on the root causes of work stress in your organisation. To do this, you need to know what the possible causes of stress may be. Here are some broad categories identified by Rosch in 'The Health Effects of Job Stress', *Business and Health*, May 1984, and developed by Kompier and Levi (1994):

- inadequate time to complete a job to one's own satisfaction;

- lack of clear job description or chain of command;

- absence of a recognition of reward for good performance;

- inability or lack of opportunity to voice complaints;

- lots of responsibility but little authority/decision making power;

- unco-operative superiors, co-workers and subordinates;

- lack of control or pride in the finished product or service;

- job insecurity due to pressures from within or a takeover/merger;

- exposure to prejudice or bigotry;

- an unpleasant physical working environment;

- worries about one's responsibilities to others;

- not being able to use personal talents and abilities;

- chances that a small lapse of attention may have serious (or even disastrous) consequences.

We will be looking at each of these potential root causes of work stress through this book.

Another way to investigate root causes of stress is to examine potential areas of conflict within the organisation. Warren and Toll in *The Stress Work Book* (Nicholas Brealey/Industrial Society, 1997) discuss this effectively. They identify key 'pressure points' that may or may not lead to increased stress amongst employees.

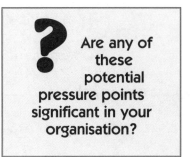

Workplace environment and conditions:

- light - is the lighting sufficient?

- privacy and space

- air freshness and quality

- resources and equipment

- standard of accommodation

Travelling:

- journey to and from work

- essential regular travelling to work within job

- adequate resources for travel (e.g. time taken recognised)

- budgets

Intrinsic to the job:

- nature of work

- overload or underload

- specific demands in the job

- extent of decision-making

Roles:

- clear or vague boundaries

- shared or conflicting expectations

- clarity of job descriptions

- extent of responsibility clear or not

Our manager:

- how we are managed

- approachable or not

- his/her own stress levels

Rewards:

- pay

- appraisal

- acknowledgement

Relationships with:

- colleagues

- manager

- subordinates

- people within the organisation

- people who influence our careers

- those we need to do the job

Our interest in work:

- levels of involvement

- satisfaction with job

- variety and pace of work

Our commitment to the goals of the organisation:

- belief in the business

- any conflict with the values or methods

Organisational culture:

- expected behaviour

- extent of communication and consultation

- internal politics and power relationships

- management style

Warren and Toll's 'pressure points' raise a lot of issues that we will deal with in later chapters. At this stage it is important that you at least give some thought to each key area.

Work carried out by Professor Cary Cooper and others, and cited in *Preventing Stress, Improving Productivity*, Kompier and Cooper, 1999, identified ten of the most important sources of work stress at a major international airport. His team used the 'occupational stress indicator' to assess a rank order for workplace stress. The finding were as follows:

Sources of stress:

1.   Working time pressures/responsibilities/overwork

2.   Pay

3.   Promotion/permanency/job security

4.   Supervision difficulties

5.   Lack of resources/staff/equipment

6.   Poor management support and planning

7.   Lack of information and communication

8.   Work environment/working conditions

9.   Feeling undervalued/receiving no feedback/no recognition for work done

10.   Overtime/shift working/working hours

Note that the order of importance given to stressors is not the same as that in the aforesaid 1985 survey (pages 23-4). This is not surprising as each organisation or industry will be different. Pay is only a stressor when it is seen to be inadequate or unfairly based.

> **?** How would each of these stressors rank in your organisation? Note that this will be a purely subjective exercise at this stage, but it might be instructive to ask your work colleagues and staff to work through the same exercise. If so, note the differences in perception between departments, rank, seniority and experience. What lessons about stress in your organisation may be learned?

In the airport example, the researchers also asked employees about stress experienced outside work - in their domestic and social life. They found that 'More than 75 per cent of outside work stressors were due to a combination of family problems relating to children, in-laws, bereavement, money problems, interpersonal relationships and recreational arrangements' (from Kompier and Cooper). This is a timely reminder that stress doesn't all come from work and that we don't always leave domestic problems at the factory gate or office reception. For your information, we will be looking at coping with domestic stress in the workplace in later chapters.

Stress auditing: how big is your problem?

4

Chapter 4

Stress auditing: how big is your problem?

What you'll find in this chapter:

- ⟱ How to discuss stress with your staff
- ⟱ Designing a questionnaire
- ⟱ What to do with checklists
- ⟱ Identifying key stress 'pressure points'
- ⟱ Creating stress charts

Stress auditing is all about where you are now and where you want to be. In the last chapter, we looked at some things you could do in the short term to become more 'stress aware'. The key is to be more aware of stress and its possible symptoms in your staff. It's all about being more observant and stress aware. In this chapter, we will look at some ways of taking a more systematic approach to stress auditing. There are several techniques on the market, but you can develop your own 'cheap and cheerful' methods that at least give you a start.

The aim of all stress audit techniques is to follow a systematic path towards understanding what stressors are likely to be affecting your staff and organisation. Most stress audits, or 'stress inventories' take the form of a questionnaire to be filled in by staff and management. These range from simple 'tick box' questions to more complex psychological profiling. The function of each type of stress audit is to create management awareness of the problem and to quantify, where possible, the likely presence and impact of the stressors at work.

One simple 'quick, cheap and cheerful' approach is to follow the advice of the Health and Safety Executive (HSE): '...get your staff to tell you about it [stress] by:

- talking and listening to them;

- asking them to describe the three 'best' and the three 'worst' aspects of their job, and whether any of these put them under uncomfortable pressure'.

note It is vital to take staff with you on any exercise aimed at discovering what is causing increased stress levels in the workplace. Failure to keep them informed may only lead to more stress.

The HSE also suggests that you 'respect the confidentiality of your staff. Tell your staff what you plan to do with any information you collect; involve them as much as possible, in subsequent decisions; involve safety representatives, if you have them, in your plans and decisions'.

I started asking my staff about stress - did they feel under pressure, were we working them too hard...some were OK but a few got really tetchy and upset at this line of questioning. They thought we were criticising them. One guy said it was really stressful having to talk to your line manager about work rates and their own health.

Ray Woodford, plant supervisor

Ray has a good point here. There is no point in adding to your employees' stress by doing things behind their back. You know how fast the rumour mill operates in these circumstances. One tyre company in Scotland almost caused a strike by asking its workforce why they go on strike. Stress auditing takes tact, care and, above all, empathy for your employees. Put yourself in their shoes. How would you feel if your boss asked if you were coping with work or felt under too much pressure? You might think you were being picked on or singled out as a slacker.

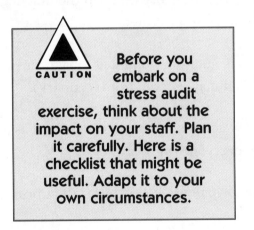

CAUTION Before you embark on a stress audit exercise, think about the impact on your staff. Plan it carefully. Here is a checklist that might be useful. Adapt it to your own circumstances.

- Plan what you intend to do and keep it under wraps.

- Work out a timetable for working on a stress audit. If this involves asking the employees lots of questions, make sure it is given in a non-stressful time, in a relaxing and non-threatening environment (the boss's office may not be the best place).

- Do not plan to hold the audit during the busiest time or when other particular pressures are at work.

- Do not pressurise staff into answering questions - it should be done voluntarily.

- Explain very carefully what you are doing, why you are doing it and the benefits it should bring to employees.

- Involve staff and their representatives (unions, for instance) at each stage of the audit. Use their ideas where appropriate. It is vital to give them some 'ownership' so that they see the process as partly belonging to them. Also, if they have had input into the design and adaptation of the stress audit, they may be more likely to co-operate.

- Make a careful record of any ideas discussed in the drawing up of the stress audit - act on them.

- Circulate details about the audit for comment - make any necessary changes (which may emerge from feedback).

- Monitor and evaluate any actions or changes suggested as a result of your audit and keep everyone on board.

- The keyword here is **involvement** - keep your staff informed and engaged.

Designing a questionnaire

The questionnaire is one of the most common methods of carrying out a stress audit. Questionnaire design is a highly complex and sophisticated business, especially when you are looking for statistical trends. Where possible, you should leave this to the experts, or invest in one of the many specialist software products that help you design questions and analyse results. There are many questionnaire software products on the market at present including the Job Content Questionnaire (JCQ) - for more information e-mail JCQCenter@uml.edu. Mercator UK also produce these products (Tel: 01454 280800) or Cambridge Software Publishing (Tel: 01223 425558).

If, however, time and money is short, there is nothing wrong in devising your own questionnaire. Although it is likely to be rough and ready, it will at least alert you to some of the issues and concerns being felt by your staff.

There are two main types of questionnaire you may consider:

1. those looking for statistically significant trends, say in absenteeism, productivity rates, accident rates, holiday backlogs (a possible indicator of overwork);

2. those that seek to elicit information from employees - to take a broad check on opinions.

As we said above, you should really leave type 1. questionnaires to the statistical experts who have experience of what size of sample to take (usually a minimum of 15); over how long to take the sample (never more than one year) and interpreting the results (both a science and an art in itself). You may need to commission a type 1. questionnaire to reveal long-term trends in stress-related problems (such as absence) or to help make a case to senior colleagues.

As for type 2. questionnaires, you can easily put together your own questionnaire on the grounds that any insight into how employees are affected by stress will be useful (as long as it is accurate).

In most cases, employees are asked to fill out questionnaires about stress during work time. There are many 'off the shelf' stress questionnaires available and they are the result of expert psychological analysis over the years.

Another commonly used questionnaire-based stress survey is the Stress Diagnostic Survey (SDS) developed by Ivancevich and Matteson at the University of Houston (see Ivancevich and Matteson, *Stress at Work, a Managed Perspective*, Scott Foreman, 1980). This is designed to help individuals identify specific stressors at the workplace and consists of 80 statements to which they have to respond (examples include 'My job duties and work objectives are unclear to me' and 'I am not part of a close knit group').

note

Professionally developed questionnaires can reveal far more than can ever be shown with a 'cheap and cheerful' home-grown survey (although this is better than nothing).

Scores are plotted to produce a stress profile of the individual. In one example given in J.C. Quick and J.D. Quick's *Organizational Stress and Preventive Management* (McGraw-Hill, 1984), a 43-year-old female administrative secretary was found to be moderately stressed due to 'rewards' and 'under-utilisation', but her primary source of work stress was due to

lack of 'career progress'. Similarly, a 56-year-old male, who was head of staff in a church, was found to have two main sources of high work stress: 'quantitative overload' and 'time pressure'.

The key point about any questionnaire is that it must be designed to discover what employees really feel and what stressful situations they face. It should not be loaded towards getting the answer the employer wants. Here are two examples of the classic 'When did you stop beating your wife' type question:

Q: 'What stresses at work are caused by your own problems?'

Q: 'Would it be less stressful if you were in a different job?'

Employees may believe that these questions are an invitation to put themselves out of a job; the likely response is either 'Don't know' or 'No'.

You should also avoid questions that the employee really cannot (or should not) answer:

Q: 'Who causes stress in this factory?'

Q: 'What should we do to reduce stress?'

The first question is far too loaded and political; the second is too broad.

Other questions to avoid are those that simply aren't going to tell you anything you didn't know before:

Q: 'Which is more stressful - work or rest?'

Q: 'Would you prefer to have less stress?'

Q: 'Do you have any family stresses?'

Q: 'Is work sometimes stressful?'

Other questions to avoid are those that are too narrow and specific to one group:

Q: 'Do you find stacking frozen fish particularly stressful?'

When designing questions for a stress questionnaire, try to keep to the following broad guidelines:

Avoid bias:

1.   Building in your own intentions and thoughts:

'You want to cut down on workplace stress, don't you?'

'Don't you agree that we have to do something about our working hours?'

'Don't you agree that stress is an inevitable part of our working lives?'

2.   Putting pressure on your staff to answer in a certain way:

'Have you tried to cut down on your drinking?'

'Do you intend to do something about your stress?'

Make your questions clear and make sure that all respondents can understand the question.

Keep it clear, simple and lacking in jargon or unnecessary technical language.

Avoid race, sex or gender bias in your questions.

Ways to start a question:

1. Asking questions about behaviour:

    'Have you ever...?'

    'Do you ever...?'

    'Who do you know...?'

    'Who does it...?'

    'How many...?'

    'In the future, will you...?'

2. Asking questions about attitude:

    'Why do you...?'

    'What do you think of...?'

    'Do you agree or disagree...?'

    'How do you rate...?'

    'Which is best (or worst) for...?'

The questions above are all 'open questions'; this gives the respondent a chance to put his or her views across. Space should be left for them to write in their responses. You may, however, wish to ask 'closed questions' - ones that can be answered only with a 'yes' or a 'no'. Closed questions are ideal for the 'tick box' format, where respondents can answer with a tick or a cross. Examples of closed questions include:

'Is your job too boring?'

'Is your working day too long?'

'Is the work too difficult?'

'Are your hours unsociable?'

> **TIP** Put yourself into the shoes of your staff and see if any question is fair, non-intimidating and useful.

You should always be aware of loading too much bias into a closed question.

Some question topics you may wish to ask:

How do you rate each of the following? (1 = poor; 5 = excellent)

- temperature in the office
- noise levels at work
- ventilation
- levels of lighting

How would you rate the standards in your office of the following?

- space to work
- cleanliness

- décor
- order

How do you rate the following facilities?

- staff toilets
- coffee machine area
- canteen
- designated smoking room
- car park
- meeting rooms
- lifts

? **This may be a good time to start thinking about your own staff questionnaire:**

- What do I need to know?

- What kind of questions will I ask?

- Who should be involved in designing the questionnaire?

- How should I keep my staff fully involved in the process?

- How can I attain support for this from my staff and superiors?

- When will I set the questionnaire?

- What will I do with the results?

And some closed questions:

'Does your job have enough variety?'

'Is your job challenging enough?'

'Are there adequate resources to do your job well?'

'Do you spend too long getting to work?'

What to do with checklists

Kompier and Levi (*Stress at Work: Causes, Effects and Prevention*, European Foundation for the Improvement of Living and Working Conditions, 1994) suggest that checklists can be used for four main purposes:

1.   to ask about job content;

2.   to ask about working conditions;

3.   to ask about terms of employment;

4.   to ask about social relationships at work.

Lesley Towner (*Managing Employee Stress in the Workplace*, Kogan Page, 1997) suggests six categories in an employee stress checklist:

1.   the culture of the organisation;

2.   the environment in which people work.;

3.   people (relationships with others at work);

4. the job itself;

5. opportunities for development;

6. implementing change.

Earnshaw and Cooper (*Stress & Employer Liability*, Institute of Personnel and Development, 1996) suggest the following questions:

'What levels of stress exist at present within the organisation?'

'Is job satisfaction, and physical and psychological health better in some areas than in others?'

'How do our levels of stress compare with those of other occupational groups?'

'Does it look as if we have a problem?'

'If we do, can we identify its cause - what appear to be the stressors?'

'Are the stressors departmental, site-specific or organisation-wide?'

They go on to suggest that checklists and further discussions should focus on:

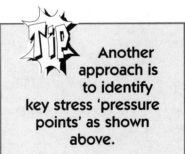

Another approach is to identify key stress 'pressure points' as shown above.

- job content and work-scheduling;

- physical working conditions;

- relationships at work;

- communications systems and reporting arrangements;

- employee expectations.

Whichever method you choose, you should ensure that the questionnaire/checklist is fully applicable to your own circumstances. It is not a good idea just to copy a checklist from others, but it is instructive to use existing checklists as a guideline. Here are two possible models, but in the end, only you can devise a checklist that fully fits your own organisation and its staff.

Stress time line

Like the seasons, workplace stress tends to come and go, ebb and flow. You will know from your own experience when stressful pressures are greater, for example in:

- certain hours in the day;

- certain days in the week;

- certain weeks in the year;

- certain years.

It is a good idea to map out a 'stress cycle' that plots key pressure points on a weekly and yearly basis.

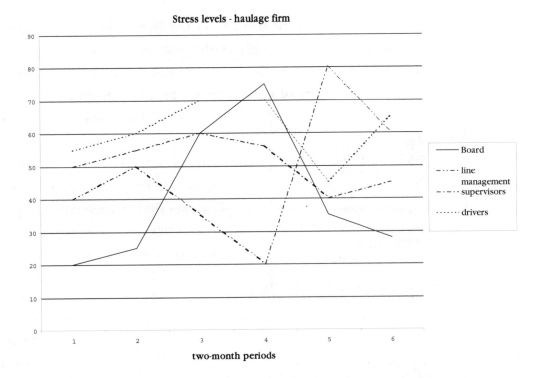

The 'stress chart' shown above as an illustration shows how different parts of the organisation experience peaks and troughs of stress at different times throughout the year.

This could be constructed by asking each group within the organisation when their times of peak stress occur. In the example above, four groups were targeted: the organisation (as viewed by the Board); the line managers (but note that not all line managers will have stress peaks and troughs at the same time); supervisors and front line drivers (again, each employee is different but general peaks and troughs could be identified by them as a group). Each group could be asked to rate their department's stress levels at each quarter, month or even week. A rating of 100 would mean, for instance, peak stress; 20-30 indicates a relatively low stress period.

This imaginary example relates to a haulage firm looking at stress levels over two-month periods throughout the year. Board members report stress levels to rise up to a peak in the fourth period - and then a gradual fall. This may reflect their pattern of reporting and business planning schedules. The stress peaks and troughs of Board members do not correlate with those of, for instance, line managers, who have their own patterns of stress. There are clear policy-making implications from understanding the nature of these differing stress patterns. You may need to give your staff some examples in this way:

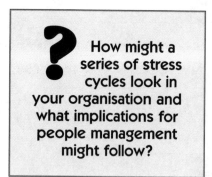

How might a series of stress cycles look in your organisation and what implications for people management might follow?

'How would you rate your stress levels for each of the 12 months in a year:

    80-100 = maximum stress

    60-80 = high stress

    40-60 = normal stress

    20-40 = low stress

    0-20 = minimal stress

Please also rate the stress levels you think are experienced in your department for each of the 12 months in a year'.

This last question can be useful - it's not just our own individual stress levels that count, but how we perceive the whole department and the rest of the team.

You may also want to ask employees why certain times are more stressful than others. For example:

'For every score more than 60, please state a reason why stress levels are so high for that month'.

This question can help to elicit all sorts of stressors that otherwise may not be obvious to you as a manager. Here are some possible responses:

July = 70: 'Summer holidays are a nightmare - keeping the children happy and looked after'.

September = 80: 'Annual stocktaking is so stressful'.

March = 70: 'End of the financial year - everyone, including the boss, feels really pressurised'.

It is also instructive to conduct your own personal stress chart - possibly on a month-by-month basis. There may be a variety of stress peaks caused by:

- annual assessment;

- monthly management meetings;

- sales presentations;

- submission of staffing plans.

My job definitely has peaks and troughs of stress. Running an English language school is very cyclical in nature. As Director of Studies, I have to plan the curriculum four or five times a year but the most stressful time is in June when I have to organise our busy summer courses (our peak time). Another pressure point is November, when I have my annual review with the school owner and present my strategic plan for the next year. This is also the time of year when we have the most staff absences through colds and flu - I spend a lot of frantic hours trying to find cover. Although it's always busy, every third Monday is a really stressful time as new students are enrolled. My quieter times tend to be in February and September.

Jane Rawsthorne, DOS at an English language school in Scotland

> **?** If you were Jane's boss, what could you do to even out her work pressures over the year? Think about writing your own stress cycle report and show it to your boss and peers. What can be done to even out the pressure load? Once armed with a stress cycle chart, you can try to plan ahead, shift resources and possibly reschedule jobs and tasks.

October used to be our most stressful month. It was the time when our order books peaked and half my marketing team were globetrotting looking for new business. It meant that a lot of strain fell on me - all I could do was fire-fight and try to keep things going.

Mark Randall, marketing manager for an Easter gifts company

'To be forewarned is to be forearmed' goes the old saying. In stress management, this is particularly true. In Mark's case, for example, one simple thing he did was to try to even out the production cycle so it didn't all fall in October. He also rescheduled the marketing calendar so that more of his team were in the office at any one time. This was done by staggering the business trips more evenly and using teleconferencing more often so that people didn't have to be out of the office so much. This was also far less stressful for his team, two of whom had small children and were especially pleased to be spending more time at home.

Getting the basics right: the physical environment

5

Chapter 5

Getting the basics right: the physical environment

There is little doubt that working conditions can significantly affect levels of actual and perceived stress in certain individuals. Physical dangers such as hazardous chemicals on site, the risk of violence or verbal abuse and poor working conditions have all been recognised by the HSE as potential stressors. Many of them are, of course, subject to stringent health and safety laws in both the UK and the European Union.

In the UK there is no specific legislation to control stress at work. But employers have a duty under the Health & Safety at Work Act 1974 to ensure 'so far as reasonably practicable' that workplaces are safe and healthy. Also, the Management of Health and Safety Regulations 1993 obliges employers to assess the nature and scale of risk to health in the workplace and to base control measures on it. Further obligations appear under the Disability Discrimination Act (DDA) 1996 that, in some circumstances, can make employers liable to prosecution if they dismiss an employee who is unable to work due to a stress-related illness.

Whatever the legal position, effective management should be about encouraging a safe, co-operative, and, where possible, happy workforce. Managers should do everything they can to remove physical obstacles to a person's psychological well-being.

If a company wants satisfied customers, the first step is to ensure the health and working environment of its employees.

Preventing Stress, Improving Productivity, Kompier and Cooper, 1999

London Transport (LT) recently introduced measures to reduce the risk of staff stress.

Using a systematic stress audit and evaluation exercise, London Transport (LT) analysed the key stressors. One of these was the threat of violent assault on station staff. They initiated a programme of training that involved handling conflict with passengers (a big issue on an over-stretched service) and other psychological pressures that affect LT staff.

Specific health and safety issues

Working with VDUs (visual display units)

Given the huge rise in the number of people working with computers, it is not surprising that attention has been drawn to the role of the computer screen or VDU in causing workplace stress. Staring at a VDU can have a physical effect on your eyesight and general health. In fact, use of VDUs is now regulated by a European Directive.

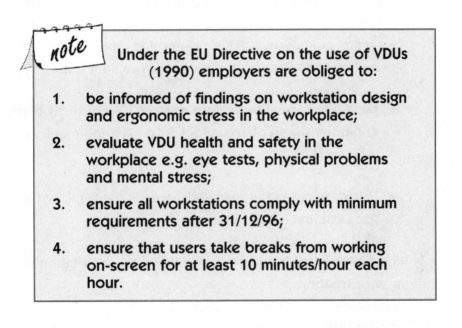

note

Under the EU Directive on the use of VDUs (1990) employers are obliged to:

1. be informed of findings on workstation design and ergonomic stress in the workplace;

2. evaluate VDU health and safety in the workplace e.g. eye tests, physical problems and mental stress;

3. ensure all workstations comply with minimum requirements after 31/12/96;

4. ensure that users take breaks from working on-screen for at least 10 minutes/hour each hour.

The link between VDU use and employee stress is less clear as the government's Health and Safety Executive (HSE) states:

People who use a VDU sometimes complain of stress, but this usually arises from increased pace of work or pressure to meet deadlines, not the VDU itself. Some VDU workers find stress reduced because the VDU makes their job easier or more interesting, but for others, the stress becomes worse. This can happen when a system does not work well or when the user does not feel in control or competent to operate it.

Employers can help overcome stress by providing the right training, and by designing systems and tasks to match the abilities of the people who work with them.

Source: HSE

In other words, the computer is merely a tool - used in the right way, it can make our lives much easier; but if things go wrong, it can be very stressful. This is especially true if the computer and its screen do the following:

- keeps 'going down' - there is nothing more stressful than losing data or having to deal with a computer program that has crashed;

- takes a long time to load up or store data - usually because the computer doesn't have sufficient power and memory to operate efficiently;

- is hard to read - because the screen is too small or there so much glare coming off the screen.

If computers are found to be a source of major irritation with your staff, find out why. Are they:

- too slow?

- too unreliable?

- too difficult to operate?

- too hot or noisy to be near?

One common way of dealing with computer problems is to 'leave it to the technicians or call out the support company'. This is fine, but persistent computer problems should be dealt with at source. You and your department could think about doing a regular annual audit of computer resources and capacities. What was fine for the business two years, or even a year ago, may well be out of date by now. If your PC or Apple Mac is trying to cope with software well ahead of its capacity to do so, you will be left with some very stressed out operators.

Apart from sheer frustration and boredom, VDU operators may report physical symptoms such as headaches. The HSE gives the following potential reasons for headaches:

1. screen glare

2. poor image quality

3. a need for different spectacles

4. stress from the pace of work

5. anxiety about new technology

6. reading the screen for long periods without a break

7. poor posture, or

8. a combination of these

Note especially number 4. What may seem to be a purely physical reaction to working with a VDU could instead be caused by the pace of work.

Installing new computing technology can often lead to a rise in the organisation's expectations of what can be done in work time. The stress this causes is compounded by poor or inadequate training and the resulting anxiety felt.

When we installed the new PCs, at first it was really exciting, but I soon started to get headaches and felt tired all the time. I tried taking pills and going to yoga classes, but at root, it was my boss's expectation that I could produce three or four times the amount of work with the new PC. On top of all that, I never really felt at home with the new system. I went to the training day but frankly, I was not much the wiser afterwards.

Bryn Morgan, data processor.

VDUs - employers have to:

- analyse workstations, and assess and reduce risks.

- Employers need to look at:

  the whole workstation including equipment, furniture and the work environment;

  the job being done; and

  any special needs of individual staff (whose views may be sought as part of the assessment).

- Where risks are identified, the employer must take steps to reduce them.

- Ensure workstations meet minimum requirements.

In Bryn's case over-expectations and poor training led to a very stressed-out employee (he subsequently quit his job and moved into outdoor work). His case emphasises the responsibility of the employer to get things right. The HSE spells out the employer's obligations under the law. See the box on your left.

These requirements are good features that should normally be found in a workstation, such as adjustable chairs and suitable lighting. They are set out in HSE's Schedule to the Regulations that cover screens, keyboards, desks, chairs, the work environment and software. All workstations now have to comply with these Regulations, to the extent necessary for the health and safety of workers (a transitional period for the modification of older workstations expired at the end of 1996).

Plan work so there are breaks or changes of activity

As the need for breaks depends on the nature and intensity of the work, the Regulations require breaks or changes of activity but do not specify their timing or length. However, the guidance on the Regulations explains general principles, for example, short, frequent breaks are better than longer, less frequent ones. Ideally, the individual should have some discretion over when to take breaks.

On request, arrange eye tests and provide spectacles if special ones are needed

Employees covered by the Regulations can ask their employer to provide and pay for an eye and eyesight test. This is a test by an optometrist or doctor. There is also an entitlement to further tests at regular intervals; the optometrist doing the first test can recommend when the next should be. Employers only have to pay for spectacles if special ones (for example, prescribed for the distance at which the screen is viewed) are needed and normal ones cannot be used.

Provide health and safety training and information

Employers have to provide training, to make sure employees can use their VDU and workstation safely, and know how to make best use of it to avoid health problems, for example, by adjusting the chair.

? • **Carry out an audit of your department's computers and screens.**

• **What do your staff think about the standard of the computers to do the job?**

• **What do your staff think about the quality of training they have received to use the computers?**

• **Are you fully complying with the law?**

• **Have you monitored the health of those people operating computers and sitting at a VDU? Does anything need to be done to improve their situation?**

• **What needs to be done to turn your department into a stress-free computer zone?**

Information should also be provided about VDU health and safety. This should include general background information. It should also cover more specific details of the steps taken by the employer to comply with the Regulations, such as the action taken to reduce risks and the arrangements for breaks.

(Source: HSE)

Other physical stressors

Many of the physical risks involved in being at work are covered by legislation. Adherence to the law (and remember that ignorance of the law is no defence), at least ensures that the worst examples of physical stress should be avoided. But adhering to the law does not mean that all physical stressors are removed. Before we look at cases within the law, it is a good idea to review briefly some of the key acts of legislation in this area. Although you don't need to know every detail, if you have an appointed health and safety manager, you should do everything possible to bring yourself up to date with current legislation and industry regulations.

You should do everything possible to bring yourself up to date with current legislation and industry regulations.

The Health and Safety at Work Act 1974 applies to all at work and in all work premises without exception. The law deals mainly with:

1. providing reasonable safeguards against risk from hazards;

2. a written policy for health and safety;

3. minimum standards of training in the use of equipment and carrying out all work duties;

4. a duty on employees to take reasonable care;

5. safety systems of work.

The law encourages you to identify potential workplace hazards such as:

- chemicals handled without care;

- electricity - loose connections and frayed cables;

- faulty ladders and scaffolding used without care and training;

- obstacles.

- plant and equipment such as fork lift trucks and cutting tools, lifting tackle;

- unguarded machinery;

- spillages causing people to slip;

- fire hazards.

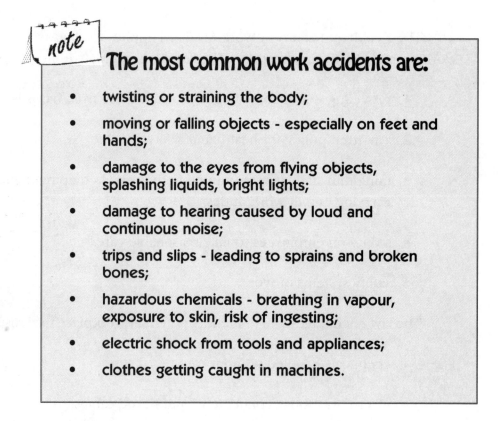

The most common work accidents are:

- twisting or straining the body;

- moving or falling objects - especially on feet and hands;

- damage to the eyes from flying objects, splashing liquids, bright lights;

- damage to hearing caused by loud and continuous noise;

- trips and slips - leading to sprains and broken bones;

- hazardous chemicals - breathing in vapour, exposure to skin, risk of ingesting;

- electric shock from tools and appliances;

- clothes getting caught in machines.

Other laws that one should be aware of include:

- Electricity at Work Regulations 1989

- Control of Substances Hazardous to Health (COSHH) Regulations 1988

- Manual Handling Operations Regulations 1992

- Noise at Work Regulations 1989

- The Fire Prevention Act 1971

- The Workplace Regulations (Health, Safety and Welfare) 1992

Although we should assume that your workplace is not in breach of the law, there are some key things you can do and check over to ensure that your workplace is a safe and pleasant place to work.

1. Keep floor areas clear of rubbish, debris, empty boxes, piled up stock and other obstructions. Close drawers, cupboard doors and locker doors. Not only does this make the workplace a tidier and more pleasant place to be, it is safer too.

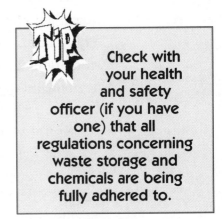
Check with your health and safety officer (if you have one) that all regulations concerning waste storage and chemicals are being fully adhered to.

2. Store and label all dangerous chemicals - from cleaning fluids to specialist chemicals used in work.

3. Ensure that the workspace is properly ventilated and there is a comfortable working temperature. Investment in air conditioning and good heating systems will pay off in terms of employee comfort. It is always difficult to get a happy medium between fresh

or cool air and warmth so think about discussing this with staff every month or so. Don't assume that because no one has complained that everybody is happy with the office or factory temperature. Getting the balance right is not easy - what is too cool for some is too hot for others. If any member of staff feels the cold more intensely, for instance, think about moving them nearer a radiator or other heat source or encourage them to wear warmer clothing. Try to avoid the 'biggest complainer gets his/her way' syndrome. It's not always those with the loudest voices who represent the greatest number of people. This is an area for common sense and a bit of forward planning. You should also check for draughts or heaters that give off dangerous fumes or unpleasant smells. The law lays down minimum ventilation requirements regarding the replacement rate of hot or stale air coming off equipment, ventilation intakes and strict rules about air conditioning systems that might lead to the lung condition, legionnaire's disease.

We had to work near the photocopier and it gave out some nasty fumes. I was really worried about it but didn't want to make a fuss.

Shona Riley, office administrator

4. Smells: Although it is easy to get used to, staff may be upset by odours given off in industrial processes. Be aware also of odours coming from outside, for example, the street or nearby factories. If this is perceived as a real problem, perhaps the answer is air conditioning and filters.

5. Space: Make sure that everyone has enough room to do his or her own work and has a bit of personal space as well.

'Our office is so cramped that you are sitting on top of each other. It's OK with people you like but there are some colleagues I would rather not be too close to.' We all enjoy our own personal space and freedom. Your office and workplace design should take this into account.

There is, in fact, legislation about workspace. The minimum space requirement for each person in an office, for instance, is 3.7 square metres of floor space. If you have a low ceiling - less than 3 metres - then the workspace per person needs to be 11 cubic metres. You need to take further guidance on this regulation (Workplace - Health, Safety and Welfare - Regulations 1992) but suffice to say that these figures should be treated as across the board averages and you should do what you can to ensure that space available is above the minimum. The rules also specify the amount of space needed for walkways, and corridors. In the end, these rules and regulations follow good common sense practice.

> Take a long, critical look at your working environment. Are you confident that your members of staff have enough room in which to operate safely and comfortably? Are corridors and aisles wide enough? Has each person got enough space to move around and do what he or she has to do (such as filing, using the telephone or PC)? Are there areas for improvement? If so, what strategies will you undertake to improve working space?

6. Lighting: Make sure that your members of staff are working in adequate and 'people friendly' lighting conditions. Again, there are

legal requirements to provide good quality lighting. The law tries to encourage employers to let people work by natural light wherever possible. This means ensuring that windows are correctly positioned, are not obstructed and are in sufficient number to allow enough light to come through. Try to avoid making your staff work in artificial light all day. You will know yourself that working under electric lights all day makes you feel isolated and oddly displaced. People like to see the sky, judge the weather (even if it means missing out on a lovely sunny day) and remind themselves that they are in the real world.

> We work all day on delivery lorry rotas but never see any vehicles leaving or arriving in the yard next door. It's a bit odd being cut off from the things you're trying to organise and it would be nice to see them coming and going.
>
> Matt Tyler, logistics manager for a supplier to burger restaurants

There are strict regulations about lighting levels (measured in 'lux' but you should check on the detail with the HSE).

7. Humidity: British Standard (BS) 7179 gives guidelines on the relative humidity acceptable where there are display screens. Low humidity is a more common problem in this country than high humidity. Low humidity can lead to various ailments including sore throats, tired eyes and general lethargy. One pleasant way to raise humidity in the office is to introduce some greenery - plants and flowers - or think about a water fountain (running water is a very soothing sound). If the problem is serious, consider buying a humidifier.

Sick Building Syndrome

Can buildings make you sick? Yes, according to proponents of 'Sick Building Syndrome' (SBS). Although SBS is not universally accepted (some experts believe it is all in the mind), others firmly believe that poorly designed buildings make people ill. For managers the issue is clear: SBS reduces worker productivity and may also increase absenteeism.

SBS is often suspected when no specific illness or cause can be identified. The complaints may be localised in a particular room or zone, or may be widespread throughout the building.

> *note*
> **Problems seem to occur especially when a building is used for something other than its original intention - a machine tool factory, for instance, converted into a set of offices.**

SBS symptoms often include headaches; eye, nose and throat irritation; a dry cough; dry or itchy skin; dizziness and nausea; difficulty in concentrating; fatigue and sensitivity to smells. The odd thing about SBS sufferers is that most feel relief soon after leaving the building.

The root causes of SBS are thought to include:

1. Chemical contaminants from outdoor sources. Outdoor air entering a building can also be a source of indoor pollution. These pollutants may come from motor vehicle exhausts, plumbing vents and building exhausts (bathrooms and kitchens). They can enter the building through poorly located air intake vents, windows, and other openings. Some pollutants may come from nearby sources (a local garage or sewage works, for instance).

2. Contamination from indoor sources. For example, adhesives, upholstery, carpeting, copy machines, manufactured wood products, cleaning agents and pesticides may emit volatile organic compounds (VOCs) including formaldehyde. Research shows that some VOCs can cause chronic and acute health effects at high concentrations, and some are known carcinogens. Low to moderate levels of multiple VOCs may also produce acute reactions in some individuals. Environmental tobacco smoke and combustion products from stoves, fireplaces, and unvented space heaters can all put chemical contaminants into the air.

3. Poorly maintained (or inappropriate) heating devices. These can produce pollutants at harmful levels. These pollutants include carbon monoxide, which is an asphyxiant, nitrogen dioxide and sulphur dioxide (SO2), all of which are irritants. These are also three of the more common products of combustion pollutants in the home.

4. Biological contaminants. Biological contaminants include pollen, bacteria, viruses, and moulds. These can breed in stagnant water that has accumulated in humidifiers, drain pans and ducts, or where water has collected on ceiling tiles, insulation or carpet. Biological contaminants can cause fever, chills, cough, chest tightness, muscle aches and allergic reactions. One indoor air bacterium, Legionella, has caused both pontiac fever and legionnaire's disease.

5. Inadequate ventilation. The race to become more energy efficient has often encouraged building designers to make their offices and factories more airtight. Reduced ventilation can lead to a host of ailments and diseases.

A recent study by Cornell University in the USA found that workers in poorly ventilated offices are twice as likely to report the symptoms of SBS as are employees in a well-ventilated environment. But their researchers found no link between SBS complaints and almost three dozen potential irritants studied, or between the syndrome and age, education, gender, general stress, positive or negative feelings or a variety of other psychological factors.

They did find, however, mild links to a variety of physical workplace problems, including sensitivity to odours, feelings of being overworked, migraines and allergies. They also found a tendency towards musculoskeletal problems. This shows that ergonomic factors are likely to play a role in SBS.

What can be done to alleviate SBS?

If you think that SBS does have a part to play in your department's well-being (or lack of it) then the solutions are fairly obvious, if rather expensive in some cases. They are:

> **?** Think about patterns of sickness in your department. Could your building be causing this sickness? You should consult with colleagues and staff on this. Consider getting an expert medical opinion before taking any action. At the very least, you should now be a little more aware of possible SBS symptoms.

- provide better ventilation. This may simply involve opening windows but not if the pollutants are coming from external sources such as a nearby toxic waste dump;

- regulate temperature in the building more carefully;

- regulate the use of perfumes, soaps, air fresheners, cleaning fluids - all of which may be irritating to some employees.

Long-term solutions to SBS may involve more fundamental solutions such as the re-design of the building. It may be necessary to get the issue of SBS discussed at the highest decision-making and budget-approving level. You may need to call in building designers or ergonomics specialists to get advice on what needs to be done.

Office ergonomics

Office ergonomics is a huge area - mostly outside the scope of this book. At root, it is concerned with ensuring that staff with sedentary, desk-based jobs do not suffer from repetitive strain injuries (RSI). Such strains and injuries are not only debilitating, but they also make people feel miserable and stressed. There are, these days, a host of companies offering solutions to RSI - from specially designed furniture to workplace exercises.

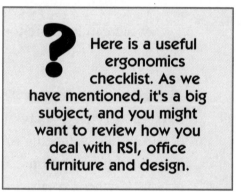

Here is a useful ergonomics checklist. As we have mentioned, it's a big subject, and you might want to review how you deal with RSI, office furniture and design.

Office ergonomics checklist

Physical checklist: posture, activity and exercise

• Maintain proper posture, paying careful attention to the positioning of head, neck/spine, arms/wrists, hips/thighs and feet.

• Alternate between different postures on a regular basis.

• When keyboarding, use minimum force while striking the keys.

- Keep a neutral wrist position, where the forearms, wrists and hands are in a straight line. Avoid awkward reaching for work tools such as telephone, mouse and reference materials.

- Avoid resting elbows, forearms or wrists on hard surfaces or sharp edges.

- Take frequent mini-breaks throughout the day to give muscles and joints a chance to rest and recover.

- Alternate between work activities which use different muscle groups to avoid overuse. Give eyes a break by closing them momentarily, gazing at a distant object and blinking frequently.

- Proper exercises are a complement to a complete office ergonomics programme. Consult with a health care professional to select appropriate exercises.

Environmental checklist: lighting, air and noise

- Maintain appropriate light levels for specific tasks. More illumination may be needed to read a document than a computer screen.

- Reduce or eliminate glare by using window shades, diffusers on overhead lighting and anti-glare filters for computers.

- Adjust the contrast and brightness on your computer screen to a comfortable level.

- Get a regular eye exam and, if necessary, wear corrective lenses. Tell your eye specialist how often you use the computer.

- Clean the computer screen and other surfaces regularly.

- Reduce the number of dust-collecting items such as papers and files on your desk.

- Use a portable air cleaner to reduce airborne particles like dust, pollen and mould. Maintain a comfortable temperature by using layers of clothing or a portable fan or heater.

- Be considerate to others working in the area and conduct meetings and conversations in appropriate areas.

- Position fabric partitions to reduce noise from conversations, foot traffic and equipment such as copiers and printers.

- Identify distracting noise and try headphones, earplugs, soft music to reduce or mask noise.

Psychosocial checklist work style: organisation and breaks

- Reduce stress by planning ahead and setting realistic expectations for what you can accomplish during the working day.

- Organise your workload to help even out busy and slow times, to avoid feeling 'swamped'.

- Vary tasks to make the day more interesting. For example, deliver a message in person instead of phoning.

- Avoid long periods of repetitive activity. For example, alternate computer work with other tasks like phone calls, filing, copying and meetings.

- Organise equipment, supplies and furniture in the most efficient arrangement for daily tasks.

- Enhance privacy by using office partitions and privacy filters for computer screens or documents.

- Acknowledge ideas and accomplishments of co-workers on a regular basis.

- Develop stress-reduction and relaxation techniques that work for you at the office and at home.

- Personalise your office with a few favourite items such as artwork, photos and plants.

- Take mini-breaks that re-energise, invigorate and refresh.

(*Source: WHALEN'S Office Ergonomics,* 139 Damon Road, Northampton, MA 01060, USA. Website: www.whalens.com)

Follow these same ergonomic guidelines at home, in meetings and while travelling.

Many of the problems of working in a confined office space can be corrected with proper seating, lighting and well-positioned monitors. But even more important is the need for people to move around during the working day. We were simply never made to sit staring at a screen for hours on end. The impact on our bodies is exacerbated by increased psychological stress that some feel.

1.   Encourage people to change positions with regular breaks involving some stretching and standing.

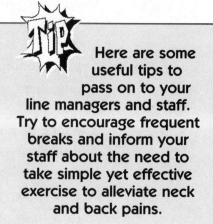

Here are some useful tips to pass on to your line managers and staff. Try to encourage frequent breaks and inform your staff about the need to take simple yet effective exercise to alleviate neck and back pains.

2.   Encourage staff to alternate tasks on a regular basis.

3.   Do some simple stretches (see below).

4.   Make sure that chairs give good lumbar support.

5.   Discourage people from cradling their telephone between their head and shoulder. This is a prime cause of neck strain.

6.   Think about buying new ergonomic office furniture.

Bringing in workplace changes is cost-effective and it benefits everybody. It's in an employer's interest to look after staff. People also think they haven't got time to make changes. But slight adjustments do make a difference. Over time smaller things have a big impact. People might not see relief in the first week or two but the aches and pains do start to go away.

Richard Sterne, co-principal of the College of Classical Massage
and Natural Therapies, Brighton

Sterne goes on to give some invaluable tips on simple exercises that can be done by anyone in the workplace. For more details see the website: www.thisisbrightonandhove.co.uk/brighton__hove/health/features/feature4.html.

People
management

6

Chapter 6

People management

Research into employee stress shows that one's role at work is a prime source of concern. An employee may feel that his or her role in the organisation is not at all clear. We all like certainty and for many of us (though not all), uncertainty is stressful. 'Knowing where I stand' is a key issue in employee relations. Here is a typical example of role conflict:

I was employed by my school as assistant caretaker. The duties were pretty clear and set out in my contract: being responsible for cleaning the upper school, locking up and leading a small team of cleaners. It didn't say anywhere in my job description that I was expected to help supervise the dinner queue or help the PTA make tea at evening events. Yet that's what the head teacher seemed to expect. It wasn't out in the open, but I just kept feeling that I was expected to do a lot more. Also, they appointed a new deputy caretaker and I didn't really know where I stood with her; who was supposed to give orders and who was supposed to be in charge. I was just getting very suspicious and felt that I was being sidelined. I eventually quit the job.

The caretaker's experience seems to be pretty typical of someone who is expected to perform a variety of roles but has never discussed these openly with his or her line manager. Role conflict and confusion is an easy trap to fall into. An organisation can often change so fast that its job descriptions become outdated. New pressures, challenges and commitments are always arising and it is not too difficult for roles to become unclear and ambiguous.

One way to avoid this problem is to ensure that when recruiting new staff, or moving existing people from one job to another, the job description should be clear and wherever possible unambiguous. This is not to say they should have a straightjacket around them. People grow and develop within a job, but their job description should be flexible enough to cope with change.

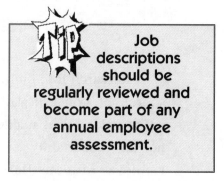

Job descriptions should be regularly reviewed and become part of any annual employee assessment.

A job description should include the following elements:

- job title;

- purpose of the job;

- objectives of the job (and in quantifiable terms if possible);

- duties expected and how these should be carried out;

- responsibilities expected - these could include:

    (i)   budgets;

    (ii)   employing staff;

    (iii)   training and development;

    (iv)   contributing to new ideas and creative changes in the organisation;

    (v)   equipment: purchase, maintenance, replacement, and operation;

    (vi)   induction of new staff;

    (vii)   team leadership or chairmanship.

- working relationships with others - whom you are expected to work with; whom you should report to; who should report to you; whom you should liaise with;

- pay and conditions including payment for extra hours or responsibilities;

- hours and holidays;

- allowances and fringe benefits.

You should also add in the job description that the employee might be asked to do other duties with reason. This flexibility is important for you as a manager but it also signals to the employee that you can't always predict what will be needed in future. You may wish to add that any extra duties will be introduced only after negotiation with the employee.

Although a clear job description is important, it cannot always do the whole job. You should also have a 'person specification' for any new post. This not only helps you and your team to recruit the right person, but it also helps to match a person's qualities and experience with the requirements of the post.

You should have a 'person specification' for any new post.

One of the best ways to reduce role ambiguity is to employ the right person in the first place.

Jack Golden, MD of a travel accessories company

The typical person specification would have the following elements:

- physical requirements for the job: health, strength, age, appearance, dress, voice, agility;

- knowledge, skills and experience;

- personal qualities looked for - these could include:

    (i)   leadership skills;

    (ii)   sense of humour;

    (iii)   ability to work with others;

    (iv)   ability to work on one's own;

    (v)   ability to work in a team;

    (vi)   creative ability;

    (vii)   administrative and organisational ability;

(viii)   self-motivation;

(ix)   even 'ability to cope with stressful situations'.

We review our person specifications for people in a post. It is useful to compare our specifications with existing staff - this helps us to evaluate their progress and to adapt the person specification for future use.

Jack Golden

The key here is to evaluate and review employment and promotion strategies. Try to ensure that your regular appraisal sessions include:

Don't forget that people grow and develop and so do person specifications. But the very process of developing a person specification can be a useful management tool.

- reviewing an employee's job description and person specification;

- ensuring that the job description is applicable for the next six months or longer;

- negotiating with the employee on any necessary changes to the job description.

This last point isn't just a one-way process. It takes two to negotiate and you should find out (a) what the organisation now requires of the person, and (b) what the person would like to add (or subtract) from the job description. This may be a delicate process (possibly involving a union or employee association) but it should not be ducked. These days, as markets become more dynamic and customers expect more, it is inevitable that job descriptions will change. Make sure you are in control of this process and not like Ken on the next page:

We installed e-mail for all administration staff last year. The result was a ten-fold increase in customer enquiries. This was good news but I hadn't really given enough thought to the impact on our staff. Though many of the younger ones took the new technology to heart, others were afraid of it. Also, the staff were just not geared to the extra volume of work now needed in replying to these customers. Some staff were upset that they hadn't had enough training in e-mail. But it wasn't just that; e-mail lets customers ask a lot more detailed questions about our services. Staff were unsure in some cases how to respond, whether they had the authority to reply to customers, and whether they should be answering every e-mail.

Ken Bryant, purchasing manager

In other words, Ken's members of staff were confused about their work role and insufficiently prepared for the changes in working practices that came about as a result of the new technology.

The lift person's job description used to say 'To operate the lift safely'. It said nothing about directing visitors to the right department, checking passes or being the first friendly face a customer might see in our building. These were unspoken, implicit parts of the job description. Now after discussing this with our staff, we incorporate all the 'extras' we expect in the job description.

Joy Messenger, office manager

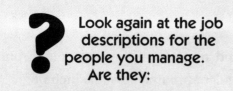

Look again at the job descriptions for the people you manage. Are they:

- clear in setting out what is expected, what goals are required;

- unambiguous - it sets out what tasks and responsibilities are expected (and perhaps gives examples);

- realistic and clearly explained targets that people are expected to reach;

- flexible enough to keep pace with changing expectations in the organisation;

- regularly reviewed with staff to ensure that role confusions have not developed. Such reviews are also necessary to find out what problems and potential stressors people have.

How do you avoid role ambiguity and role conflict? The simplest and most effective way is to have a structured interview between staff and supervisor or manager. You could ask your staff questions such as:

Describe to me your own job tasks:

- What do you think is expected of you in this job?

- What resources or information do you think you need to do the job well?

- What areas of trouble or difficulty do you think will or may occur as you begin the job (or develop a new job responsibility)?

(Adapted from Ivancevich and Matteson, Stress at Work, a Managed Perspective, Scott Foreman, 1980)

The problem, of course, with this type of interview is that employees may only tell you what they think you want to hear. The only answer is to work at creating (or developing) a more open style of management. This means creating an open and honest climate where people are not penalised (or think they may be penalised) for speaking the truth.

 One way to encourage people to tell you their job role and any worries they have, is to ask open-ended questions. So instead of asking, 'Are you happy with your current job?', try instead, 'Which aspects of your job do you find most satisfying, or most difficult?'

Recruiting the 'wrong person' for the job can be a prime source of stress - for both the employer and employee. In recent years, there has been an increasing reliance on psychometric testing to ensure that the right people are recruited and that the process identifies any training and development issues.

The theory behind psychometric testing is that role conflicts can be avoided and that there is a much closer 'fit' between the employee and his or her work. The tests are used not only in recruitment, but also for internal staff development. Proponents of these tests argue that testing an employee will show up strengths and weaknesses which affect the way people work, and the way they operate in teams. If people are in the 'wrong job' or trying to do things that are against their nature, they can become stressed and anxious. They don't perform well and are not generally happy in their work.

There are many psychometric tests on the market. One of the oldest and most established is the McQuaig word survey, first devised in Canada in the 1940s and now used widely throughout the world.

The word survey employed by McQuaig identifies four basic temperament traits:

- Dominance (D)

- Sociability (S)

- Relaxation (R)

- Compliance (C)

People identified with a 'High D' score, for example, may be competitive and highly goal oriented. A person with a 'Low S' score may be work-oriented, an analytical thinker and a good planner. Someone scoring a 'Low C' may be independent, strong minded and determined. The McQuaig survey provides a character assessment where people have a mixture of traits. Here are two possible examples:

A person with a High D but Low R score is likely to be highly competitive, goal oriented and ambitious. The Low R also means that he or she has a strong drive towards goals.

A person with a High S but Low D score is likely to be sociable, outgoing, friendly, optimistic, expressive and a real enthusiast; very animated and a 'life and soul of the party' type.

The McQuaig survey helps to identify people as either 'Generalist' or 'Specialist'. In the extreme, a 'Generalist' is interested in the whole picture, looks at the wood not the trees, can see component parts and how they fit together and looks for a challenge. He or she wants responsibility for an entire project.

Also in the extreme, a 'Specialist' is peaceful, co-operative and will follow instructions. He or she is a good team player, works well under supervision and likes to concentrate on one area at a time.

Of course, all manner of variants between these two poles are possible in the survey outcome.

One aim of a psychometric test like McQuaig is that managers can assess a person's strengths and limitations in terms of:

- forming and developing a team;

- handling change;

- rising to new challenges;

- developing skills and new responsibilities.

Psychometric tests can be a useful tool in the manager's armoury. They can help you to fit the best person for the job and anticipate problems and issues of change. They can also help design the most effective training and development paths. If, for example, an employee is found to be an 'Enthusiastic Generalist', this is likely to mean that he or she is very outgoing and friendly, independent and determined. But that person is also likely to make emotional decisions based on feelings rather than facts. Careful analysis and methodical problem solving is not their way. That person, according to the McQuaig survey technique, is not likely to be very happy working in a routine, facts-oriented task. Putting that person in such a work role will make them unhappy, frustrated and stressed.

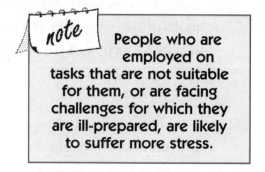

note

People who are employed on tasks that are not suitable for them, or are facing challenges for which they are ill-prepared, are likely to suffer more stress.

Psychometric tests and surveys have been described as 'fitting square pegs into square holes'. Though this is an over-simplification, there is some truth in the fact that their use is primarily to ensure that people are well suited to what they are expected to do. Used professionally, these tests may also help you to train and develop your staff in such a way that they are more prepared for new challenges and opportunities, and are better able to face the inevitable changes that affect most working lives these days.

Some psychometric tests also focus on a person's ability to learn and adapt to new situations. One example is the McQuaig Occupational Test (MOT), which measures a person's ability to think quickly. The MOT tests vocabulary, verbal reasoning skills and the ability to perform simple mathematical functions. Like many well-established psychometric tests, the MOT enables an employer to make subtle judgements about a person's potential. By testing vocabulary, verbal reasoning skills and the ability to perform simple mathematical functions, the MOT gives guidance on how a person is capable of thinking. It is a rough measure of a person's capacity to grasp new ideas.

Like all psychometric tests, the MOT and word survey are part of the manager's toolkit. They are useful pointers and are there to enhance your own intrinsic management skills (not to replace them). Stress and anxiety are likely to arise from employees who are 'square pegs in round holes' - they are expected to carry out a task or responsibility for which they are ill-suited (although training and development can enable them to rise to the challenge of change).

Advantages in using psychometric tests include:

- They often encourage organisations to do a thorough job analysis in order to identify appropriate skills and abilities.

- They can increase the likelihood of being able to predict future job performance.

- Tests can enable the comparison of individuals in an objective and fair way.

- They can help to overcome the cost of selection errors.

- If used properly they can reduce staff turnover by identifying training needs.

- Tests can improve staff motivation in order to take individuals to their full potential.

Disadvantages:

- They can be expensive in terms of time and money.

- Employers may come to over-rely on them - they are not a substitute for good interviewing and communication skills.

- Some may be unproven - the buyer must beware.

> **?** Does your organisation use psychometric tests to help recruit new staff and develop existing ones? If not, do some research to see what tests are on the market and consider how they can help to ensure a closer fit between the individual and the job role.

Dealing with conflict

One important cause of role confusion and ambiguity is poor or ineffective handling of conflict situations. As a manager, you will no doubt have to handle conflict between you and your staff; your staff and colleagues; and your staff and customers or suppliers. Failure to handle conflict successfully is a key source of stress in many organisations. Much of this comes down to the perception of role and individual assertiveness. Here are some typical quotes (how many of them seem to apply to your job as a manager?):

'The one thing I really hate about my job is dealing with conflict. I much prefer the quiet life.'

'I try to avoid conflict at all costs. That's OK for my staff but it puts a lot of stress on me.'

'If I'm criticised by a line manager, colleague or even a customer, I tend to let it really get me down. I carry it around for weeks going through in my head how I should have dealt with it and what I should have said or done.'

'My senior manager is very bluff. If I make a mistake, he gets very personal. You come to live with the insults but it's not easy to handle'.

The management, or mismanagement, of conflict is a clear source or organisational stress. Handling conflict in a stress-minimising way is very much an issue of clarity and good communication. To ensure this, take note of the following:

- Roles should be clear.

- Expectations should be clearly communicated and not implicit.

- Lines of authority should be well established and transparent.

- Conflict-resolution procedures should be clearly in place.

- Conflict at work should never become personalised.

In my old, non-assertive days, I used to dread conflict of any kind. I'd do anything to avoid an argument. It was partly because I didn't believe in myself and also because I hated people being unpleasant to each other. Now I see that conflict can, if handled properly, be a good thing.

> Andrew Chalmers, MD of a publishing company

Do you try to avoid conflict at all costs?

People who try to avoid conflict are often non-assertive, rather passive types. Similarly, those who always seek conflict tend to be overbearing, aggressive people. There is a middle way. Conflict can be creative, provided it is dealt with assertively, and that means no winners and losers but everyone gaining something.

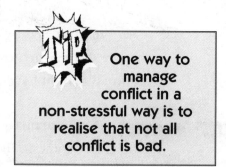

One way to manage conflict in a non-stressful way is to realise that not all conflict is bad.

Conflict can be a good thing because:

- it can stimulate new ideas;

- it can lead to better team work;

- it provides a reason for discussion, debate and analysis;

- it can provide a useful safety valve for all sorts of pent-up emotions;

- it keeps people on their toes.

None of this means that conflict needs to hurt people. As an effective manager, you should seek a 'win/win' not 'win/lose' situation. In other words, one person's gain should not be at another's loss.

I used to have a boss that loved stirring things up. He seemed to thrive in an atmosphere of argument, recrimination and tension. The trouble is that no one else did. The rate of staff turnover was high and sickness and absenteeism were rife.

Andrew Chalmers

Conflict can also be fun. A lot depends on how well you know your colleagues or friends. Light-hearted joshing is quite common in the workplace and people don't tend to get upset by it when there is a sense of mutual respect and good feeling. Where there are fierce rivalries and old scores to settle, conflict can be very dangerous.

Managing conflict - golden rules

- Take control in a conflict situation. Watch out for other people being hurt.

- Never personalise - let debate and discussion flow freely but don't let this become an attack on an individual.

- If you are in the middle of a conflict and very unhappy about it, be honest and say so. Say that there needs to be a different way of resolving the arguments. Challenge others to settle the conflict without resorting to personal abuse or negative attitudes.

- Tell people that conflict, which doesn't lead to some kind of improvement for all, is a waste of time, energy and money.

There is nothing more destructive than bottling up your feelings. A colleague at work once made me look very foolish in front of my line manager. I've never said anything but I've been harbouring a grudge for years. I still go through endless mental debates: what I should have said or done, what I could still do to get my own back. The trouble is, whenever I see my colleague, I pretend that nothing is wrong.

Terry Newman, works supervisor

Bottled-up emotions are harmful. They make people resentful and broody and they keep them awake at nights with the injustice of it all, gnawing away at their self-confidence.

Does any of this sound familiar?

- You still remember, and resent, a comment that someone made about you years ago.

- There's something you really want to tell your family but can't face up to it.

- You want to ask your boss for promotion but can't face him or her.

- You suddenly 'snap' and become angry about something that happened days or weeks ago.

- You often think, 'If only I'd said this or that at the time'.

These examples are typical of passive behaviour. Even aggressive people tend to bottle up their emotions at times. Being assertive is about having the self-confidence to express these emotions. There are very good reasons for expressing your feelings:

- It makes you feel better - less depressed, less paranoid and less likely to have a sudden, angry outburst.

- You can bury an old argument.

- You can put the conflict behind you and start to make progress.

- It should lead to better human relations.

Bottling up feelings gets a person nowhere. It's also true that it is not always a good idea to 'let off steam'. An angry, uncontrolled response can:

- make things worse by upsetting other people;

- make you look foolish;

- make enemies;

- prevent you from learning from the situation.

If you feel upset by someone's remarks or criticisms, don't delay; tell them what you feel and why you feel unjustly treated. Write down your thoughts, taking care to edit out any aggressive or abusive sentiments.

> **TIP** Handling conflict in an assertive way is neither about bottling up feelings, nor does it mean reacting instinctively every time. It does mean taking control of the situation.

When you are happy with your written response, write it out again as a memo, note or letter. If you prefer, use it as guidance notes for a face-to-face meeting with the person who has upset you. Do the same for any long-standing grudges. Write a letter saying that you would like to meet again and outlining why you have felt upset for so long.

I always used to blame myself for situations at work. If there was an argument, it was always my fault; if there was a report to write, I knew it would go wrong; if there was a presentation to give, I knew I'd make a mess of it.

Derek Cowling, sales manager

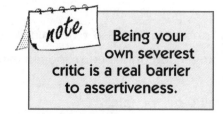
note Being your own severest critic is a real barrier to assertiveness.

How can other people respect you when you don't respect yourself? Passive people are very good at making a crisis out of nothing. They arrive at meetings, interviews, presentations, discussions, etc. so wound up that they often make a mess of things. This is a typical example of 'self-fulfilling prophesy'. You are so sure something bad is going to happen that you behave in such a way to make your worst fears come true.

Here are some typical fears that non-assertive people may have at work. How many apply to you as a manager? Then think about the people you manage - how many of these apply to them?

- fearing the worst - about the results of an interview or sales pitch;

- a dread of being appraised - fearing that you will be 'found out' or seen to be lacking in some way;

- avoiding all conflicts;

- believing that everyone else is cleverer or smarter than you;

- being afraid of making mistakes.

These common features of the passivity are often caused by:

- feelings of inadequacy;

- thinking the worst will happen;

- trying to prepare for the worst;

- wanting to avoid conflict;

- setting unrealistic expectations.

These negative feelings can best be tackled in three simple ways:

1. Banish negative thoughts and work out (on paper if necessary) a strategy for being and sounding positive. The old adage 'energy breeds energy' has a sound basis.

2. Set realistic and achievable targets for you and your team.

3. Challenge your own inner voice on each negative point. Tell yourself what you can do, rather than what you can't do.

Criticising others

One of the most difficult aspects of my job is criticising my staff. I hate doing it and sometimes I lie awake the whole night before, working out what I'm going to say, and how I'm going to say it.

Frank Baker, personnel director

It is (or can be) very difficult for a non-assertive person to criticise others. The reasons are:

- fear of upsetting people;

- fear of an angry reaction;

- fear of being wrong.

The essential point about criticising other people is that you should be targeting their **behaviour** and not them as people.

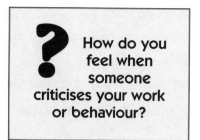

Criticism is often an essential fact of life. If you honestly feel that a job or task falls below expectations, then you should say so. Never bottle up criticism.

The skill of assertiveness is to know how to criticise behaviour without personalising it. Criticism should never:

- belittle the person;

- make them feel upset or inadequate;

- cause a heated argument;

- lead to a fight;

- be used just to get things off your chest;

- become a style of management ('I also have a go at my staff as it keeps them on their toes').

The role of criticism is to make things better - to put things back on course to success. Criticising someone is not worth doing, if it doesn't lead to an improvement. It is a very risky business. As you saw from the last section, people can bottle up old grievances and perceived slights for many years. This isn't to say that criticism should never be used. It is an essential tool of progress, if used correctly.

- Criticism of others should always be positive. Always say what can be done to improve next time.

- Never criticise others when you are feeling angry - wait, calm down and work out how to make progress.

- Choose the right place and time.

- Always be calm, in control and honest about how you feel.

- Give the other person a chance to have a say.

- Steer the conversation away from blame - that is totally non-productive.

- Get the situation into perspective - was the error or mistake made really so important?

- Be prepared if the other person gets upset - don't continue until they feel in control.

- Ask the other person for ways to improve the situation.

- Follow up any criticism with a summary of what has been decided.

- End on a friendly or at least non-aggressive note.

Taking criticism

Even as a mature adult, I find it hard to cope with criticism. However justified it is, or thoughtfully presented, I can't help feeling it's a personal attack.

Derek Cowling

How do you respond to being criticised?

- I feel guilty.

- I defend my position whatever.

- It really upsets me.

- I'd do anything to avoid it.

- I like a good argument.

- No one would dare.

These are all either passive or aggressive responses. The assertive and therefore less stress-inducing way to receive criticism is:

- to accept that the other person has the right to criticise your actions;

- not to accept that the other person has the right to criticise you as a person;

- to accept constructive criticism and see it as a learning experience;

- not to accept insults or abuse but to stand your ground calmly and honestly.

Encouraging your team to accept positive criticism

- Try to encourage them to welcome criticism as part of their personal development.

- Always ensure that everyone has a say in working out what happens as a result of the criticism.

- If the other person gets abusive or angry, say 'I'm sorry, but this sounds more like abuse than genuine criticism'.

- Do not tolerate any kind of personal attack. Say that you do not think it necessary, appropriate or in any way constructive.

- Be prepared to give your own side of the story and listen to others.

- Encourage everyone to give his or her version of events.

- Don't encourage people to make vague criticisms - insist on specific examples and set that as a standard.

- Remember your body language as you are being criticised - sit up, or stand very straight and look the person in the eye (but not aggressively). Don't shuffle but maintain a calm pose of a person in control. If necessary, make notes or ask for a representative to be at the meeting.

- Avoid being 'hijacked' by someone who has had adequate time to prepare the criticism. Be prepared to ask for time to prepare your response.

Ten ways to take and give criticism

1. Tell yourself that conflict can be a very good thing - don't always try to avoid it.

2. Take control in any situation where there is conflict or criticism. Don't be passive or aggressive.

3. Never tolerate personal abuse.

4. Tell people that conflict or criticism that doesn't lead to some kind of progress is not worth having.

5. Write down your feelings if you would rather not confront someone face to face.

6. Criticise others in a positive way, giving them a chance to contribute.

7. Avoid blame - it won't make things better.

8. Receive criticism as a learning experience.

9. If being criticised, ask for specific examples of where and how you went wrong, and what should have been done.

10. Insist on being criticised at a time that suits both parties. Make sure you prepare for the session.

It isn't easy but criticism should not be confused with personal attack or abuse. The latter is always negative and just leads to long-term grudges and upset. Positive criticism is actually essential in any organisation that wants to move ahead. Welcome criticism and be prepared for it.

Saying 'yes' when you mean 'no'

I've always found it hard to say 'no' - especially when friends or work colleagues ask a favour. It must be the way I was brought up. I consider it really rude to let someone down. What I didn't realise was how much of my time I was giving up to please others.

John Harris, catering manager

> **note**
>
> Saying 'yes' when you mean 'no' is a typical symptom of passivity. It means ignoring your own views and wishes in order to meet someone else's objectives. This is passive behaviour and can be an important source of employee stress.

Many people, managers and staff included, find it hard to say 'no' and to refuse to do a job or obey an instruction that they don't feel is right. Doing something we do not believe in is a potential stressor. And yet many people see it as their role to obey instructions regardless of what they feel. As a stress-aware manager, you should be attuned to what people think about their work.

But many people find it hard to say 'no'. They see it as letting someone down or appearing to be rude.

It is perfectly possible to learn to refuse requests in an assertive manner - in other words, to respect your own wishes without having to score a victory over someone else. The three key principles are:

* honesty - with others and, even more importantly, with yourself;

- self-respect - your rights are just as important as the other person's. You have a right to say 'no';

- communication - being able to share with the other person the reason why you have to turn down a request.

Once people know that you always agree to any request, you'll find yourself being exploited and overworked. It's as if your time isn't as valuable as theirs.

Gavin Jenkins

If I say 'no':

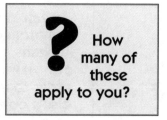

- other people will get annoyed with me;

- other people will be let down by me;

- I am being rude or selfish to people;

- I'm getting rather 'above' myself;

- I'll find it more difficult to ask them for a favour in future;

- I will be unpopular.

All of these thoughts are typical of the passive person. Let's look at some reasons why you should think more assertively when asked to do something.

Fear of saying 'no'	Assertive viewpoint
People will get annoyed	They should respect my feelings
People will be let down	It shouldn't be 'you win, I lose'
I'm being rude	It all depends how you say it
I'm not important enough to say it	You are just as important as the others
Asking for favours in future	If there is mutual respect and you have been honest and direct in saying 'no', then it shouldn't be a question of 'tit for tat'

What are the consequences of passively saying 'yes'?

- You get the reputation of being a 'doormat'.

- You are overworked and stressed.

- You harbour hidden resentments about the people who have asked you to do things.

- You may eventually lose your temper and control.

- You are tempted to become more aggressive, which is as destructive as being passive.

How to say 'no'

Saying 'no' isn't just about using a two-letter word. It's very important to know how to say it without offending or letting down someone else. And even more importantly, you have to say it and know why you've said it.

Gwen Littlewood

It is part of good people management to encourage your staff to be assertive and honest. Part of this openness and honesty is their ability and confidence to say 'no' or, at least, 'let's think about this decision'. Much of this will depend on the climate and culture in your organisation. Sometimes, of course, the person who has to say 'no' is you.

Saying 'no' to the boss

It's never easy to do this. You always feel that saying 'no' may well jeopardise your chances of promotion. In fact, as the MD of a medium-sized company, I can say that I much prefer honesty. I also prefer an employee to tell me that a job can't be properly done than have to accept second best. I'm honest with my staff, and I want them to be honest with me.

Linda Barnes, MD of a printing firm.

? Assuming that you have a boss, do you find it hard to say 'no'? Think of the reasons why this might be so:

- I might lose my job.

- I might lose his or her trust.

- I'm too scared to say it.

- Surely it's my job to do as he or she asks.

These are all passive, or non-assertive, responses. Remember, your subordinates may be thinking the same thing about you. It is too easy to believe that compliant and respectful members of staff are all working away happily. But underneath, these responses may show a lack of self-respect or worth.

Here are some useful reasons for starting to manage your boss more effectively, and that means learning to say 'no' now and again.

It's in your boss's interests to:

- make sure you stay fit and well - asking you to do too much can damage your health;

- keep you employed (if you're doing a good job);

- know what you really think - how else can he or she make the right decisions?

- treat his or her employees well.

But what if you have a really intimidating boss?

Put your refusal in writing but ask for a follow-up meeting if further explanation is required.

Ask for time to consider the request and in the meantime send a short summary of all the other work you have to do.

Redesigning the job

7

Chapter 7

Redesigning the job

'My job is naturally stressful - there's nothing you can do about it.'

'Stress is what we pay people to experience in this business - the old adage 'if you can't stand the heat, get out of the kitchen' applies to us.'

How often do you hear these views, especially in the business world? There is often an assumption that stress 'goes with the job' and there is little that can be (or even should be) done. Many people believe that stress is a positive sign that an employee is working hard. But as we have seen, stress can be a destructive element in the workplace. Stress is not always an inevitability. What is certain is that a poorly designed job, or one that takes little account of the psychological health of employees, will lead to higher levels of stress than is necessary. Think of this as avoidable stress.

> *note*
>
> **Psychological studies have shown over the years that there is a positive correlation between levels of stress (as measured in quite specific health terms - heart disease, for instance) and the way a job is designed.**

One of the key issues seems to be 'decision latitude' - the ability of an employee to have some influence over:

- how to perform a work task;

- when that task should be carried out;

- what skills and talents should be developed in the workplace.

Many research studies over the years in psychological and sociological fields have shown a negative relationship between employee health and decision latitude. In jobs where people have little or no say in how they carry out their tasks, the levels of heart disease and other stress-related ailments seem to be higher. It appears that the level of demand placed on an employee is far less important in creating psychological stress than the amount of decision latitude he or she has. In other words, a job where demands are very low (both in mental and physical terms) can be very stressful for some employees if they have little or no say in their work. Here is an example:

I worked for three years as a receptionist in a furniture factory. It was so boring. There were few visitors each day and my duties were very light. OK, I could take in a book to read and was mostly left to my own devices, but the thought of spending eight hours a day in such a tedious job would make me ill. I took a lot of days off sick and eventually quit.

It seems that any job can be stressful if the employee has little or no say in how it is carried out. This isn't universally true, of course, and the key rule is to know your staff well.

My job is a real cinch. I've got it down to a fine art, with minimum thought and action. I love it because I spend all day dreaming and thinking up stories which I then write up in the evenings. Being in a boring job really suits me.

This last example may be something of an exception. It seems that most of us like to have a say in how the job is designed. But a crucial element to 'democratising' job design is to give an employee full support.

We could design our own shift rotas and work out who does what each day. That was good because it gave us a feeling of being in control. We even had a say in ordering stock and pricing up snacks. I suggested that we bought in free newspapers for customers and had lots of good music in the background, which we chose. The trouble was that if things went wrong, we'd get no backing from management - you got yourself into this, now get yourself out, was their attitude. It meant that in the end, we were too scared to suggest anything.

Rob Levinson, 19 year-old barman

note Decision latitude without support is pretty useless in combating stress. It's like saying, 'I give you the independence to make a decision but I don't want to be implicated if things go wrong'.

Two secrets of good job design seem to be:

- Give employees some decision latitude.

- Support them in making those decisions by offering advice where sought, and back-up if and when things go wrong. Support should not be on a trial basis. It's of little use to say, 'You can make your own decisions but if things go wrong, you lose that right'. This is hardly a good basis for building employee confidence in their own decision-making abilities.

> **?** How much independence do you give to your team in making decisions about what they do, how they do it and when they do it? Could you give them more autonomy and, if so, what issues would face you if you did so? These might include implications for the budget; training and skills development; organisational structure and hierarchy and communication channels.

Remember, that to devolve decision-making downwards involves a degree of delegation. We will look at this issue in more detail later.

Job enrichment

Another way to improve employees' motivation is to enrich their job experience. This may mean a fundamental change in the way a job or series of tasks is done but, in some cases, only a small adjustment to the modus operandi is required. Frederick Herzberg, who contributed to human relations and motivation in terms of organisation development with his two theories 'Hygiene Theory' and 'Motivation', found, in his work on motivational factors, five strong determinants of job satisfaction:

1.   achievement

2.   recognition

3.   the work itself

4.   responsibility

5.   advancement

Oddly enough, Herzberg, in his seminal study of a cross-section of Pittsburgh industry, found a completely different set of factors that brought about dissatisfaction at work. These were:

1.   company policy and administration

2.   supervision

3.   salary

4.   interpersonal relations

5.   working conditions

What Herzberg found was that the absence of the five 'satisfiers' is far less likely to cause worker upset than the presence of any of the five 'dissatisfiers'. He labelled the satisfiers as 'motivators' and the 'dissatisfiers' as 'hygiene factors'. His view was that each job has specific hygiene factors that relate to the environment in which the workers operate (the working conditions including, for instance, lighting and heating, salaries and employee benefit programmes). Herzberg's view was that if an organisation failed to provide adequate hygiene factors, then employees would feel significantly dissatisfied, as absence of a hygiene factor may cause upset and stress.

The quality of supervision is without doubt a key concern. Training in human resource management should be at the forefront of any supervisory training programme. But all too often, supervisors are trained in technical skills without the ability to deal sensitively with staff issues.

> **TIP** How would you rate the people management skills of the supervisors who report to you? Is there a training need here and if so, what actions are needed to bring this about? If it is not already a part of your staff assessment programme, you should consider this aspect of a supervisor's work role.

Job enrichment means, in effect, adding more depth and breadth to a job. This may mean more autonomy for the team; it may also mean more emphasis being placed on achievement and recognition of contributions made by staff. Such recognition needn't be very involved and can range from a mention in the staff newsletter (perhaps in an 'Employee of the Month' award) to tangible rewards in the form of bonus payments or incentive trips. One recent trend has been for companies to take employees out on weekend 'team building' or 'networking' events. Here is one recent example:

Three teams from Bristol's 'Bacon & Woodrow' office spent the weekend in Castleton competing in a tribal extravaganza with teams from offices across the country, as well as from Germany and Holland and some unsuspecting clients. In all, 180 took part and the event was designed and organised by Bristol based consultancy, 'Interaction Development & Learning Consultancy Ltd.'

Leading actuarial consulting firm 'Bacon & Woodrow' staged the event as part of their change strategy promoting better working relationships, multidisciplinary working and innovation. Each team or 'tribe' competes for basic resources and progresses to the evolution of an interdependent community that trades, works and has fun together. The underlying message is clearly to promote collaborative rather than competitive team working.

Friday began with orienteering. Participants were handed basic survival gear, a map and a very cryptic cornish pasty that happened to contain a clue of six small-lettered stones. Actors were positioned around the village and each team had to find ten characters, find out their names and gather 'basic resources' from the area. These characters included 'Lord Thaarg', who was to be found in the local castle holding court, and a 'jilted bride', who was positioned on a hillside playing her violin. Despite the wet conditions, all had great fun. One character bearing a sign saying, 'Hungry, homeless and mute' was actually offered a barn for the night by a local farmer!

Saturday was spent half in the moors learning all sorts of 'survival skills' ranging from lassoing, whip cracking and juggling to abseiling for food (chocolate eggs) and totem-pole building. Then it was back to base camp to play tribal drums, to face-paint with natural pigments and to a whole host of circus skills. By the afternoon, each team was dressed in their own tribal costume and made their way to the great Peak Cavern for a candlelit drumming and chanting, followed by a procession through the village back for feasting, cabaret and partying.

Sunday morning was designed with hangovers in mind and began with a hike up into the hills, followed by a trading exercise that many enthused was the most enjoyable part of the weekend. All things active ended with an 'Olympiad', which involved an elaborate cart race, crawling through tunnels constructed from bales of straw and all sorts of obstacles to climb over, through and under. Exercises demanded a mix of creativity, mental agility and physical ability and prizes were given to the best team in each category. The elaborate and complex scoring system, devised by one of the actuaries, received an award in itself. Two of the Bristol teams made it into the top seven with one winning a prize for the highest score in mental agility.

According to Martin Laws, associate actuary at the company, 'Exhausted but elated is the best description of the people from the Bacon & Woodrow Bristol office who took part in last weekend's Challenge 2000 in the Peak district. There was something for everyone - from running through the forest at night looking for clues in streams to taking part in tribal drumming sessions, from juggling on the moor to learning how to throw a stage punch. The weekend gave everyone an opportunity to do something different and to meet and compete with colleagues from all over the country.

Many companies, large and small, are now considering such motivational events rather than, say, giving a cash performance bonus. The long-term benefits can be much greater in terms of staff attitudes. According to the company organising the above event, clients find a real and measurable benefit in organising these events in terms of:

- retaining staff;

- team bonding;

- co-operative working;

- client networking.

 Although the design of such events needs to be very carefully matched to the interests of staff, there is growing evidence that incentive and motivational trips (even afternoon events) can have a long-lasting impact on staff morale.

Successful and effective delegation

Delegating power and control is never easy but it should not involve the delegation of authority and responsibility.

I've just had a month off work due to what, I suppose, was a mild nervous breakdown. Things were really getting to me at work. I just seemed to have more and more to do. I couldn't sleep, I kept late hours at work (even went in most weekends) and things got really tense at home. Looking back, I could easily have delegated much of the work (so much of it was routine). Why didn't I do it? Fear and guilt, I suppose. I thought it was my job to get these tasks done. I also felt I couldn't trust my subordinates to do a good job. The result was that everything fell on my shoulders.

Graham West, warehouse manager

Graham's problems are typical - overwork caused primarily by poor organisation. Delegating work means organising your time more effectively. But to delegate well, you have to believe in what you are doing. Here are some of the things that delegation is not about:

- doing less work;

- shifting responsibility on to others;

- ducking your own responsibilities;

- tricking people into doing your work.

In other words, delegation is not about shirking your responsibilities. It is about sharing responsibilities.

Delegation checklist

Do I need to delegate?

Look at the checklist below. If two or more of the statements are true for you, chances are that you really need to delegate more effectively.

- I often feel overworked.

- I often have to take work home with me at the end of the day or at weekends.

- Subordinates are always coming to me with problems that I feel they should really be able to deal with themselves.

- If I do delegate work to others, I'm always worrying if it's going to be done properly.

- I sometimes spend a long time checking and correcting tasks that I've delegated to others.

Effective delegation means that you are able to pass on tasks to others with the confidence of knowing the job will be well done. Also, as a skilled delegator, you will be able to pass on delegation techniques to your staff. Delegation should be seen as a cascading of decision-making. The problem is that once a task is out of your hands there is always the nagging fear that things will go wrong.

I'd love to delegate more to my staff but I'm really reluctant to do it. The reasons are simple. Firstly, I feel guilty about others doing jobs that really should be mine. Secondly, I feel that my staff are hard pressed enough without me giving them extra work. Thirdly, I've had one or two disastrous attempts at delegating important work to others. One time, a member of my team forgot to turn up to a vital sales meeting that I normally attend. Lastly, I'm a bit ashamed to say it, but deep down, I feel that if I delegate too much work to others, I might spoil my chances of promotion. It's important for the boss to know that I'm doing a good job, not my assistant.

Bill Hayter, showroom manager

Common reasons for not delegating are:

- guilt - 'I'm paid to do this, not my assistants';

- trying to be helpful to subordinates, i.e. 'not giving them too much to worry about';

- fear of your staff making a complete mess of the job delegated to them;

- fear of being blamed when things go wrong;

- fear that the boss will think less highly of you if you are not seen to be doing all the work.

Delegating is not always easy. Like many things in business, it is more of an art than a science. The first step to successful delegation is to recognise why it sometimes goes wrong.

Knowing what to delegate

It's a common irony of life at work that you are often so busy with day-to-day tasks that you cannot see how to make your job easier. Perhaps you would like to delegate more, but new tasks keep coming in and everyone seems so busy that there just isn't time to think about who does what. Instead, it's much easier to do it yourself.

TIP The first person you need to convince about delegating is you. So think carefully about why you want to delegate more tasks. Make a list of three or four good reasons why you should delegate more - you may have some 'selling' to do to convince others of the benefits of delegation.

This is a very common trap to fall into and it's not always so easy to get out of it.

The first step is to plan to set aside some time to analyse your job more carefully. This may have to be done outside work hours or maybe one weekend (if you ever get one).

Make a list of tasks that seem to take up so much of your time.

1.   Make as full a list as possible. Think about last week or month.

2.   Divide the list into jobs/tasks that take under 15 minutes/ between 16 and 30 minutes/longer than 30 minutes.

3.   Against each item on the list, think of other people who could do those tasks for you.

The reason for listing short jobs is that added up, they can be major time stealers. They are often the mundane, routine, repetitive jobs that could be certainly done by junior or subordinate staff.

Set aside half a day to work out all the tasks you normally complete in a month (this will be time very well spent).

Think about the tasks that you want to delegate, and those you want to (or have to) keep for yourself.

Assign some of the delegated tasks to subordinates (but be careful how you 'sell' the idea - see below).

Selling delegation to your staff

'One man's delegation is another's extra burden.'

'Delegating tasks to others can be a sensitive business.'

I decided to delegate all my more mundane and repetitive tasks to my two assistants. I decided who should best do what and sent them a memo stating their new tasks. Of course, I was a bit worried about their ability to do the jobs so I asked them to report all their work to me once a day. The result of this exercise was that two perfectly charming and co-operative assistants became irritated, rather embittered souls who seemed to resent my every order. So much for delegation.

Anne Baxter, MD of a printing company

Anne's experience is an object lesson in how **not** to delegate tasks to staff. She:

- only delegated the boring jobs;

- failed to discuss these with her assistants first;

- left it to an impersonal memo;

- gave a signal to her staff that she didn't even trust them to do a boring job and, as a result, they felt undervalued and overworked.

Delegation should be seen as 'empowering' staff. Genuine delegation means that you share some of the responsibilities that you would otherwise have. Delegation does not mean getting others to do things you don't want to do yourself.

To help promote greater delegation to your staff, present the delegated tasks as:

- a challenge;

- a sign that you trust in your subordinate;

- a career opportunity.

Delegating tasks involves getting others to accept responsibility. It means that you have to **trust** your subordinates.

Think about some of the tasks you currently do that could be delegated to others. What qualities should you look for in a person who can be trusted with a task you would normally do yourself?

You might be looking for a whole range of qualities. These could include qualities that others share with you or qualities that others have that you do not.

Knowing to whom to delegate is all about knowing your staff, their strengths and weaknesses and what their capabilities could be.

Delegation is not an absolute. There are degrees of delegation ranging from delegating nothing and expecting no initiative at all to devolving every one of your current tasks to others. In between these two extremes lies a range of options. Here are some:

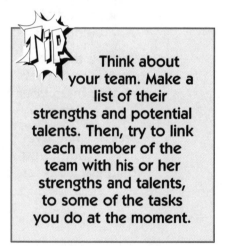

Think about your team. Make a list of their strengths and potential talents. Then, try to link each member of the team with his or her strengths and talents, to some of the tasks you do at the moment.

- Subordinates wait to be given orders.

- Subordinates have some discretion to do certain tasks - but must ask permission.

- You recommend a course of action and leave it to the subordinates to act.

- You leave the subordinates to decide what course of action to take but ask them to report each result back to you.

- Your subordinates can take what action they think best and only need to report to you on a routine basis.

Delegation does not always mean giving up all involvement. There are degrees of delegation that fit different circumstances:

- You bring in your staff and consult with them on a course of action, but you make the final decisions.

Carry out an audit of your staff's strengths and potential talents.

Choose the best person for the job and give them your full support.

Decide what level of delegation you would like to offer.

- You join a team of subordinates as an equal voice - the team makes a collective decision.

- You allow your subordinates to form their own team who are given authority to make decisions.

When you are ready to delegate more tasks to your team:

- Make sure that your subordinate knows what the end result of the task should be.

- Be clear about the level of initiative you expect and how little, or often, you expect the person to report back to you.

- Have some method of assessing the results of the task.

- Make sure that you 'sell' the benefits of delegating the tasks (see above).

- Once a task is delegated, don't keep interfering.

- Delegate to the next level down - don't skip, as it will create a lot of bad feeling.

- Make sure that you have given your subordinates enough support and the resources to do the job properly - this may involve some training time but it's a good investment.

- Delegate interesting and useful jobs.

- Reward your subordinates for carrying out delegated tasks well.

Well-managed delegation not only eases the burden on you and your colleagues, but it also helps to give your staff a sense of commitment and involvement. Delegation, as we have seen, is not only about shared responsibility, but it is also about ownership. Ownership of a task is likely (in a well-managed organisation) to reduce the incidence of stress. It does this partly by encouraging consensus. Employee stress is created by having to work at tasks employees don't believe in. It also arises from the employees having no part in creating a set of tasks. 'Consensus' and 'ownership' or 'stake-holding' may be buzzwords for the 21st century, but they do have an important part to play in the psychological health of your workforce.

Conflicting demands

Unless you are working in a very small organisation, you are likely to be one of several managers, each, on paper, with particularly defined responsibilities. In theory this is fine but in practice, areas of responsibility can easily become blurred and boundaries too often overstepped. Ill-defined management responsibilities can be another source of employee stress. Here is an example:

You never know who to listen to in this company. One day my line manager tells me to do one thing, and on another, his boss tells me to do something else. The other day I had an instruction from my supervisor to clean out the storeroom ready for a new consignment. When the manager got to hear about this, he went mad as I was supposed to be finishing off the paperwork on a really important order. I'm always getting stuck in the middle and I don't know half the time who I should be listening to.

Bev Nicholson, warehouse assistant

TIP Is it possible that your instructions to staff are being contradicted by other members of the management team (and vice versa)? Talk to your staff and colleagues about this. The first stage is to be aware of the problem. If there is a problem, you should work as a team in making sure that the lines of authority are clearly re-established and that staff should know to whom they are responsible.

Conflicting demands are a consequence of an organisation whose management structure has become rather blurred. There is no easy solution to this but the first stage is to recognise when this is happening. Staff may be reluctant to talk about the problem, fearing that they are stepping on the toes of several managers. But if your members of staff are complaining about unclear or conflicting orders, you should investigate and discuss with your management colleagues how well (or badly) your lines of authority are working. It may be something to discuss with your employees, their union or association. It is important that managers appear to be working in harmony and towards the same goals.

In an organisation where delegation and empowerment of decision-making is common, there should be fewer opportunities for conflicting demands. There should also be a climate where members of staff are better able to understand why certain (perhaps unpopular) decisions are being made.

In delegating tasks and responsibilities, it is essential that people be given sufficient resources to carry them out to the best of their abilities. 'Resources' in this context can mean the money and facilities to do a job properly. It is no use delegating a task that the employees will find impossible to do in the circumstances.

> When we delegate tasks, we delegate budgets. The two always go together. They must.
>
> MD of a large multinational company

> We run a small voluntary organisation. Demands on our time and help are increasing all the time. The problem is that we don't have the money to meet those demands so it's getting ever more stressful.

This last quotation is typical of the situation for many voluntary organisations, where demands are growing but resources are not. As organisations are being increasingly 'downsized' or 'rightsized', there is an increasing pressure on people down the line to do more with less. 'Leaner and meaner organisations' may look good at top management level, but down at the 'shop floor' it may mean people having to work much harder on tasks they don't understand or support. It also means that people are often doing jobs that they have not been trained for, or ever wanted to do. All of this is a sign not of efficient downsizing, but poor and weak management.

Another consequence of flattening or 'de-layering' management structures is that employees have fewer places to fall back on when things are tough. In the past, organisations have often been able to dissipate ill-feeling, tension and staff disillusionment through complex bureaucratic structures. Strong combative trade unions were able to take the pressure off employees by fighting for them; individual managers could always call on a many-layered structure of authority where big problems could be delegated upwards. Nowadays people often feel more exposed. They have to fight their own battles and stand up for

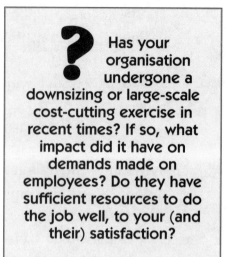

Has your organisation undergone a downsizing or large-scale cost-cutting exercise in recent times? If so, what impact did it have on demands made on employees? Do they have sufficient resources to do the job well, to your (and their) satisfaction?

themselves across functional boundaries; they need to be more assertive advocates of their own position. But if they can't easily stand up for themselves, stressed staff may seek to project problems on to other individuals or groups. In a flattened organisation, stress and conflict may be more out in the open.

Job redesign

The nature of the job is often seen as a key stressor in organisations. People may be dissatisfied with their role because it fails to stimulate them, or they cannot see the relevance of what they are doing or have little stake in doing it well. Whilst training and better management communication have a role here, there may come a time when the best long-term solution to workplace stress is the fundamental redesign of a job. The benefits in terms of greater autonomy, employee satisfaction and increased motivation and creativity are worth the investment it may take. Individual creativity is built on one's role and position in a stable organisation where employees feel empowered to make new suggestions, contribute ideas for improvement and even design their own jobs (either as individuals or members of a team).

Job redesign - where to begin?

If you feel that a job requires a redesign or makeover, then the starting point is to analyse the job in terms of:

1. what tasks need to be completed (or taken to a desirable outcome)?

2. how significant are these tasks? What impact do they have on the aims and objectives of your organisation? It is surprising how many tasks are carried out simply because no one has analysed their usefulness. 'We have always done it this way' is a common cry. As a manager, you should look critically at every job you are responsible for. Why has it always been done that way and is it the best way?

> **List all the jobs done by your staff. How well would each rate in terms of the five points above? You could assign a score to each one where 1 = very poor and 5 = excellent, for instance. If a job scores (say) less than 14, you may want to look at it as a candidate for redesign.**

3. what skills and talents are needed to carry it out?

4. what degree of freedom and autonomy does it grant the person carrying out the job? Is there another way of achieving objectives; doing a job differently that would give employees more autonomy?

5. what level of feedback is enjoyed by the person carrying out the job? Does he or she get any sense of why they are doing it, or a feeling of gratification or satisfaction? Is there recognition for doing a job well (and not merely a system for punishing poor work)? For so many jobs, there is a one-way feedback or broken loop. If a job is done badly, there is recrimination and blame; if it is done well, nothing is said.

The exercise above is for general guidance only. You may find that a job scores well on all but number five - feedback. But that one area of weakness is sufficient to make people very dissatisfied with the job. You must use your own judgement here (and that of your peers and staff).

How to redesign a job

In their book *Organizational Stress and Preventive Management*, Quick and Quick quote JR Hackman's five principles for task redesign. They suggest that one of these five principles may be used to change a job. These principles are:

1. Form natural work units - organise people into work groups or teams.

2. Combine tasks - de-specialise a job and allow individuals to do several different activities.

3. Establish client relationships - enable workers to interact with internal or external customers.

4. Use vertical loading - allow workers more responsibility and discretion over what they do each day.

5.   Open feedback channels - increase the ways in which feedback from the work process may be made more open and available to workers, so that they are better informed and feel part of the decision-making process.

In effect, these five principles involve managers in:

- forming or developing and strengthening team working;

- job rotation and enrichment;

- improving customer care;

- increased delegation and worker autonomy;

- improving management communication.

Team building

Many books have been written about the formation of close-knit and effective teams. A full investigation of this issue lies outside the scope of this book but we can point to some key issues and actions that you, as a manager, may wish to think about.

How can you build a successful team within your organisation? It is all about planning and knowing a bit about the dynamics of the team. A strong and charismatic leader is not always the best catalyst for the profitable team. Sometimes it is best to lead from behind. Team building involves trust and delegation. It is not always an easy thing to do. Here are some characteristics of the poor team leader. Does it sound familiar?

The poor team leader:

- treats the team as a bunch of underlings ready to take orders;

- expects every team member to be equally skilled or committed to the task;

- sets his or her own goals and objectives for the team to achieve;

- rarely, if ever, consults members of the team;

- sits back and waits for results.

Team building is an art - a real human skill. If done well, building a team can be enormously rewarding - for the working environment and your bottom line. Here are some useful team building tips:

- Clarify the role and purpose of the team.

- Recognise that it takes time (and resources) to build a good, cohesive team.

- Know your team. Try to find out as much as you can about the individual strengths and weaknesses of each team player. Respect people's limits.

- Help (but never bully) the team into dividing tasks and roles so that individuals concentrate on what they do best.

- Recognise that not everyone has equal skills. Some team members are good negotiators; others are strong on technical issues, human resources, finance, forward thinking and creative planning (see below on Belbin).

- Define team roles very carefully but be prepared to be flexible about these and any time constraints.

- Make sure that every team member feels valued and is able to participate.

- Ask yourself, 'Am I the best team leader?'. You may find that someone has a real skill in chairing meetings, in summarising arguments, in finding common ground in moving the team onwards.

- Work hard at improving your communication skills. Remember, a good team builder is a great listener.

note

One of the key skills of any effective team manager is the ability to look for signs that things are going wrong. Teams are organic entities. They develop their own personalities, moods and tensions. The problem with team stress, however, is that it can have a domino effect. It only takes one member of the team to suffer from work-related stress for that to spread like a virus. The old adage that a chain is as strong as its weakest link is all too true for work teams. One person who feels depressed and stressed may perform poorly. In a close-knit team this may mean that others have to bear the burden of this one person. What was once harmonious and positive collaboration becomes fractured and argumentative. It is not unusual in these circumstances for the burden of extra stress to fall on team leaders (or those who are most conscientious). Instead of creative energy, there is destructive and wearisome conflict, argument and bickering. In these circumstances, office politics can become much more potent than the power of the team to meet organisational objectives.

How to spot a team beginning to break down. Look out for:

- people missing meetings or coming in late;

- an atmosphere of mistrust;

- normally positive and enthusiastic team members wanting to leave;

- deadlines missed;

- formation of little cabals;

- lack of focus at meetings;

- increase in gossip;

- formation of destructive alliances;

- lack of direction and a tendency for 'meetings drift' - team meetings that only succeed in generating more meetings.

Watch out for any of these tendencies. They are signs that the team is not working well and may be caused by one or more members feeling stress or general malaise.

? What can you do to build a team out of staff who are used to working on their own? Or what can you do to strengthen an existing team?

As we have seen, building a successful team means knowing about the strengths and weaknesses of each member. Employee stress happens when people are forced to do things they are not able or happy to do. Successful team building is about recognising individual skills, talents and (perhaps above all) potential. It's your job as an effective manager to recognise the potential in your team, and help to develop that to the full.

Much has been written about team formation including Bruce W. Tuckman's seminal work (see 'Developmental Sequence in Small Groups', *Psychological Bulletin*, Volume 63, 1965) on the four stages of team development: forming, storming, norming and performing. There has also been a wealth of research on group dynamics and team personality types such as the work done by Meredith Belbin (see *Team Roles at Work*, Butterworth-Heinemann, 1993). He identifies key team players as:

- Chair: co-ordinator

- Shaper: team leader

- Plant: innovator or creative thinker

- Monitor-evaluator: critical thinker

- Company worker: implementer

- Team worker: team builder

- Finisher: detail checker and pusher

- Resource investigator: researcher

Belbin's questionnaire method seeks to identify strengths in these roles so that team members are placed and encouraged in areas where they can do most good. The general view that teams are better than individuals works in many cases, but a team has to be an effective one. It is an interesting debating point to argue that an ineffective team is worse than leaving people to their own devices. Tuckman's work (and others) has shown that the initial stage of team formation, called 'forming', is absolutely crucial in setting the right tone and mood for building effective teamwork. Forming a team is like testing the water: how will people get on? Will personalities collide? Will a team leader emerge who will be respected and listened to? Will everyone get a chance to shine? Can team differences be exploited in a positive way?

Here are some simple guidelines for building effective teams.

1.   Make sure that the aims and objectives set for the team are clear and measurable. The team should know why it is in existence.

2.   Make sure that team members are very clear about their task roles and responsibilities. Clarify all boundaries so that people also know what they should not be doing.

3.   As a team leader, make sure that everyone gets an equal chance to participate - even those who are naturally more introverted.

4.   Make sure that team members don't feel in competition with each other - watch out for bruised egos and career ladder climbers. You should always try to get on top of the 'office politics' that goes with any team.

5.   Set clear lines of communication so that crossed wires and mixed messages don't get sent. The more open your team, the more they will trust each other and internal communication will be all the

more effective. But also make sure that the team communicates effectively with the outside world.

6.   Be aware that all teams suffer stresses and strains after initial enthusiasm and euphoria. Watch out for 'team burn-out', where members cease to support each other and look out only for their own interests.

Improving customer care

Helping staff to feel more in touch with clients and customers (whether internal - people within the organisation who rely on them to do their work well - or external), not only helps the bottom line, but it can also act as a key motivator. For some (but not all) people, having contact with their clients can actually be de-stressing. This is because:

• you can see how and where the product or service you produce is being used;

• you can get satisfaction from knowing that the client is happy with what you are producing for them;

• dealing with clients involves personal contacts and can make a job far less isolating;

• being in contact with clients helps to produce a sense of pride in what you do.

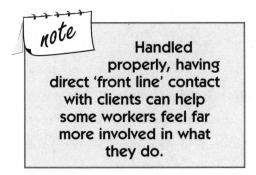

note

Handled properly, having direct 'front line' contact with clients can help some workers feel far more involved in what they do.

Absence of involvement is a key stressor for many people. But, of course, you have to beware that client and customer contact requires a great deal of tact and skill. Ill-trained or unsuitable staff can feel far more stressed if they have to face clients (especially if the clients are difficult to handle or are having lots of problems).

Front office work where you are face-to-face with clients can be very motivating, but it can, for some, be a high risk factor - especially if insufficient training is given. There is also an issue of 'fantasy customer care', where people go through the motions of giving good service but as soon as the boss' back is turned, go badly off key. How do you prevent this?

Consistent customer service is all about ownership and personal motivation. It all comes down to management style. Assuming you have recruited the best people, it's a question of encouraging staff to feel that excellent customer service is something they feel proud to offer. The staff must 'own' good customer service standards. This means you must consult them on how to improve and maintain customer care. One approach is to focus on the drive, attitude and confidence of staff. Drive puts in the will to use the skill and also makes for happy members of staff that get a sense of achievement from their working day.

The Quality Circle approach can yield amazing dividends and managers should encourage staff to come up with their own ideas to provide great service. Quality Circles were popular in the 1970s and 80s and involved small groups of five to fifteen people from the same work group. They met regularly (often weekly) to discuss quality issues and to consider how products and services could be continually improved. The aim was also to put quality on the agenda with a wide group of workers.

Here are some basic tips to help improve commitment to customer care:

- Illustrate publicly your own commitment to customer service - be a shining example to clients and staff. In other words, lead from the front.

- Treat your staff as if they are your customers too - they will pass to clients what they receive from you.

- Constantly praise good staff performance - to encourage your team's pride in the service they give.

- Regularly seek staff ideas on improvements to customer service - involvement breeds personal responsibility.

- Reward these ideas - it will encourage far more to emerge.

- Seek constant feedback from customers - share with staff and implement service improvement ideas.

- Train your staff in 'people skills'. In fact, consider whether you need training in these skills too.

Appendix

Dealing with the symptoms of stress

Many organisations deal with employee stress by offering on-site services, or access to off-site treatments and care. Although this is dealing with the symptoms of stress rather than the root causes (which is what this book is really all about), it is worth considering if there is anything your organisation can do to ease the many and varied symptoms of stress among employees.

There is increasing use made of so-called 'employee assistance programmes' (EAPs) which organisations are buying into in increasing numbers. These can be thought of as bought-in welfare support services. Typically, a large firm employing 1,000 people might pay around £25 per employee per year to access a range of EAP services. These usually include a 24-hour telephone or e-mail helplines (dealing with problems such as finance;,legal issues or work-related concerns such as redundancy or harassment). Having free access to these helplines that are staffed by trained counsellors and advisors is designed to encourage people to seek help and assistance in a very confidential way. If a problem turns out to be quite serious or the caller is deemed to need extra assistance, the helpline staff can suggest telephone counselling or even face-to-face counselling from trained practitioners recognised by the British Association for Counsellors. The companies that provide EAPs should be members of the Employee Assistance Professionals Association (see p151 for the contact details for both of these organisations).

If a fully fledged EAP is out of the question, there are still many things that can be done but remember, it is always better to offer stress-related assistance in a confidential, non-threatening way. Here are some ideas you could try:

- Hold regular (two or three times a week for instance) relaxation sessions in the lunch hour or after work. A trained practitioner who is skilled in the arts of yoga, deep breathing and other similar practices should lead these. There are also a lot of relaxation or self-hypnosis tapes on the market that could be available in a quiet area of the building (or even borrowed by staff to take home).

- Encourage staff and employees to take part in more sports and recreation activities. Sport is excellent for team building and should be very enjoyable (but don't add another layer of stress by organising highly competitive team games). Many organisations have membership with a local tennis or golf club with discounts for staff or perhaps you could think about striking a deal with a local gym, fitness centre or swimming pool.

- Think about employing a welfare officer (could be part-time) to be on hand to discuss employee concerns. Failing that, get yourself trained up in counselling or mentoring skills. However, it is usually better if the welfare officer is an outside person.

- Counselling should not be presented as a cure for some sickness or an admission of personal failure. This needs to be handled with great sensitivity. Make sure that the manager responsible for organising the counselling sessions has great skills of tact, diplomacy and discretion.

It is true that stress at work is part and parcel of modern living. There is even something good to be said about it. But stress can be destructive, harmful, oppressive and miserable. A stressed out workplace is no fun to be in. Given that unmanaged stress makes your workforce unhappy and less productive - and given that we all want a quieter and more enjoyable life at work - it is time to take the bull by the horns. Start managing stress before it manages you!

Encourage staff and employees to take regular breaks and to eat a healthy diet.

Useful addresses

British Association for Counselling and Psychotherapy, 1 Regent Place, Rugby, Warks CV21 2PJ. Tel: 0870 443 5252; Fax: 0870 443 5160; E-mail: bac@bac.co.uk; Website: www.bac.co.uk.

British Psychological Society - Register of Competence in Occupational Testing (RCOT desk), St. Andrews House, 48 Princess Road East, Leicester LE1 7DR. Tel: 0116 254 9568; Fax: 0116 247 0787.

CIPD produce a booklet on using and selecting psychometric tests. To order, contact **Chartered Institute of Personnel and Development**, CIPD House, Camp Road, London SW19 4UX. Tel: 020 8971 9000; Fax: 020 8263 3333; E-mail: cipd@cipd.co.uk; Website: www.cipd.co.uk.

Employee Assistance Professionals Association, Premier House, 85 High Street, Witney, Oxon OX8 6LY. Freephone: 0800 783 7616; Fax: 01993 200401; E-mail info@eapa.org.uk.

Index

Headings relate to stress and employment, the principal topics of the book.

F

H

I

J

MADE EASY books available from Law Pack...

Look out for the Professor! Made Easy Guides are practical, self-help business reference books which take you step by step through the subject in question.

- Legal and business titles
- Experts' advice
- 'How to' information and instructions
- Save professional fees!

Business Letters I & II

Business Letters I and Business Letters II are complementary Made Easy Guides, each providing an invaluable source of more than 100 ready-drafted letters for a range of business situations. Each letter has a useful commentary which helps you choose the right turn of phrase. The Business Letters Made Easy Guides take the headache and time-wasting out of letter writing, and provide you with letters that get results.

Code B504	ISBN 1 902646 38 X	PB	
250 x 199mm	142pp	£9.99	1st edition

Code B505	ISBN 1 902646 39 8	PB	
250 x 199mm	152pp	£9.99	1st edition

Negotiating Tactics

What business can expect success without being able to negotiate good deals? In today's competitive world, you need to know about the tactics and techniques which professional negotiators use to win. Negotiating Tactics Made Easy pools the expertise of 12 experienced negotiators and is packed with advice and tips on handling almost any situation. Be prepared for the ploys and techniques you are bound to come up against!

Code B507	ISBN 1 902646 45 2	PB	
250 x 199mm	234pp	£9.99	1st edition

To order, visit www.lawpack.co.uk or call 020 7940 7000.

MADE EASY books available from Law Pack...

Limited Company Formation

Incorporation as a limited liability company is the preferred structure for thousands of successful businesses. Limited Company Formation Made Easy Guide explains why, and shows you how to set up your own limited liability company easily and inexpensively. It provides detailed but easy to follow instructions, background information, completed examples of Companies House forms and drafts of other necessary documents.

Code B503	ISBN 1 902646 43 6	PB	
250 x 199mm	112pp	£9.99	1st edition

Profitable Mail-Order

Mail-order business is big business, and it's growing year by year. Setting up and running your own mail-order business can be fun as well as profitable. This Made Easy Guide shows you how to do it, explaining the vital importance of product profile, building valuable mailing lists, effective advertising and a whole lot more. It divulges the mail-order secrets that ensure success!

Code B510	ISBN 1 902646 46 0	PB	
250 x 199mm	206pp	£9.99	1st edition

Running Your Own Business

You have a business idea that you want to put into action, but you also want advice on the realities of setting up and running a business: this Made Easy Guide is for you. It takes you through the business-creation process, from assessing your aptitude and ideas, to funding and business plans.

Code B511	ISBN 1 902646 47 9	PB	
250 x 199mm	140pp	£9.99	1st edition

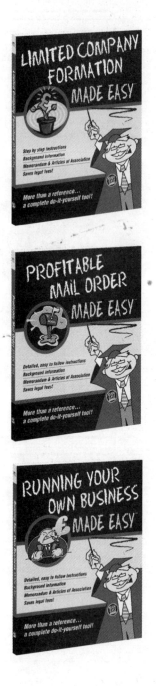

To order, visit www.lawpack.co.uk or call 020 7940 7000.